BEYOND PSALM 150

Discover More Sacred Songs of Praise, Petition, and Lament throughout the Bible

PETER DEHAAN

ISBN:

978-1-948082-70-9 (e-book)
978-1-948082-71-6 (paperback)
978-1-948082-72-3 (hardcover)

Library of Congress Control Number: 2021923306

Published by Rock Rooster Books, Grand Rapids, Michigan

Credits:

Developmental editor: Kathryn Wilmotte
Copy editor/proofreader: Robyn Mulder
Cover design: Taryn Nergaard
Author photo: Chelsie Jensen Photography

To Laura Alexander

Contents

Celebrating Scripture's Other Psalms

Paul writes to the church in Colossae that they are to teach and admonish one another with psalms, hymns, and spiritual songs, singing with grace in their heart to the Lord (Colossians 3:16).

He writes a similar sentiment to the church in Ephesus: "Be filled with the Spirit, speaking to one another in psalms, hymns, and spiritual songs; singing and making melody in your heart to the Lord" (Ephesians 5:18–19).

The book of Psalms feels like an ideal place to start this quest.

Some people think of the Psalms as a collection of Hebrew poems. I like that. Others call it a prayer journal. I like this perspective too. Just as our prayers cover a range of styles and emotions, so do the Psalms. We can have Psalms (and prayers) of praise, lament, thanksgiving, and so forth. Some Psalms burst forth as a corporate hymn, while others seep out slowly as a personal prayer of anguish.

Whatever our mood or perspective there's likely a psalm that captures our emotion and our heart. It's no wonder, then, that people over the centuries have so treasured the Psalms.

The range of content addressed by the Psalms covers a wide array of themes. Bible scholars attempt to classify the Psalms by topic, but there's little agreement in their groupings. The labels they use include hymns, laments, thanksgiving, praise, compassion, liturgy, prophecy, petition, and so on.

Yet not all the Bible's psalms reside in the book of Psalms. Other psalms occur throughout Scripture from Exodus to Revelation. This book collects these randomly located passages to make it easy to find them and to immerse ourselves in them.

Compiling this list of psalms scattered throughout Scripture has been a time-consuming yet stimulating task. To create this list, I looked for passages of song and poetry that provided personal or community prayer and worship. This book contains those passages, with sixty-seven more biblical psalms for us to contemplate, commiserate, or celebrate. As we do, may God receive our attention and adoration.

Some of these psalms appear in paragraph form instead of as poetry. This is because of the translation used, not because these passages aren't biblical poetry. Regardless of the format, embrace each one as a psalm.

Given that Psalm 151 is in the Septuagint (a Greek translation of the Old Testament from the original Hebrew, used in Jesus's day), we'll start our numbering of these additional psalms at 152. This is for convenience and structure, nothing more.

In exploring these other psalms scattered throughout the Bible, we'll use the World English Bible (WEB) as our text. It's based on the revered American Standard Version of 1901 and updated for today's readers. Notable in the WEB is the use of the Hebrew name Yahweh (or sometimes just Yah) instead of Lord or Jehovah. It adds a sense of awe, connecting us today with our faith's Hebrew heritage.

[Most versions of the Bible are under copyright, which prohibits their use in this book. The WEB, without copyright restrictions, is the ideal option for our exploration.]

Psalm 152:

Song of Moses

Exodus 15:1–18

Psalm 90 is the oldest chapter in the book of Psalms. Moses wrote it. Though it's his only entry in the Psalms, Moses penned other songs as well, but we need to search for them. We encounter one in the book of Exodus. Though we don't know when in his life Moses wrote Psalm 90, this passage in Exodus likely came first.

Moses and the people have just left Egypt and head toward the promised land. Blocked by an uncrossable sea before them and chased by the pursuing Egyptian army behind them, they have no path for escape. Death is certain.

Yet God miraculously rescues them. He divides the sea so that his people can cross the space before them on dry land and reach the other side. When the Egyptian army follows them across, the waters crash upon them, and they perish.

God saves his people from certain death, and Moses writes this psalm in praise to Yahweh.

"I will sing to Yahweh, for he has triumphed gloriously.
He has thrown the horse and his rider into the sea.
Yah is my strength and song.
He has become my salvation.
This is my God, and I will praise him;
my father's God, and I will exalt him.
Yahweh is a man of war.
Yahweh is his name.
He has cast Pharaoh's chariots and his army into the sea.
His chosen captains are sunk in the Red Sea.
The deeps cover them.
They went down into the depths like a stone.
Your right hand, Yahweh, is glorious in power.
Your right hand, Yahweh, dashes the enemy in pieces.
In the greatness of your excellency, you overthrow those who rise up against you.
You send out your wrath. It consumes them as stubble.
With the blast of your nostrils, the waters were piled up.
The floods stood upright as a heap.
The deeps were congealed in the heart of the sea.

The enemy said, 'I will pursue. I will overtake. I will divide the plunder.
My desire will be satisfied on them.
I will draw my sword. My hand will destroy them.'
You blew with your wind.
The sea covered them.
They sank like lead in the mighty waters.
Who is like you, Yahweh, among the gods?
Who is like you, glorious in holiness,
fearful in praises, doing wonders?
You stretched out your right hand.
The earth swallowed them.

"You, in your loving kindness, have led the people that you have redeemed.
You have guided them in your strength to your holy habitation.
The peoples have heard.
They tremble.
Pangs have taken hold of the inhabitants of Philistia.
Then the chiefs of Edom were dismayed.
Trembling takes hold of the mighty men of Moab.
All the inhabitants of Canaan have melted away.

Terror and dread falls on them.
By the greatness of your arm they are as still as a stone,
until your people pass over, Yahweh,
until the people you have purchased pass over.
You will bring them in, and plant them in the mountain of your inheritance,
the place, Yahweh, which you have made for yourself to dwell in;
the sanctuary, Lord, which your hands have established.
Yahweh will reign forever and ever."

Reflection: Think about a time when God miraculously protected you from danger or harm. This moment may have been epic or perhaps it felt small, but either way your life took a different path as a result.

Did you praise God for his deliverance then? Take a moment and do so now—or do it again.

May we revere Yahweh as he works in our lives.

Psalm 153:

Song of Miriam

Exodus 15:21

The shortest chapter in the Bible is Psalm 117. It weighs in at a mere two verses, serving as a reminder that our efforts to praise God need not be long or wordy. Sometimes succinct is better. Miriam's song of praise to God, only one verse long, is a reminder that less can be more.

Miriam responds to Moses's praise of God's amazing rescue with a psalm of her own. Moses's older sister picks up her tambourine and leads the women in dancing before Yahweh. In doing so, this prophetess stands as the Bible's first worship leader.

> "Sing to Yahweh, for he has triumphed gloriously. He has thrown the horse and his rider into the sea."

Reflection: We should praise God to the best of our abilities and according to how he has equipped us. The quantity of our worship doesn't matter, only that it comes from our heart.

Does our praise to God sometimes feel like it's less than the efforts of others? Remember that none of us can fully praise God to the extent that he is worthy. Therefore, it's foolish to compare our worship to that of others.

Without considering other people's actions, what can we do today to praise God for who he is and what he has done?

May our acts of worship focus on God, without giving thought to what others do or say.

Psalm 154:

The Nation Sings

Numbers 21:17–18

As the people of Israel travel about in the desert, water is scarce. They reach the city of Beer. God instructs Moses to gather the people, and he will provide water to quench their thirst.

The people respond collectively, praising God in song. Though this seems like a poem to the well that produced the water, let's understand this as an indirect praise to God for guiding them to the water that the well provided.

All praise rightly goes to God, from whom all blessings flow—including water.

> "Spring up, well! Sing to it,
> the well, which the princes dug,
> which the nobles of the people dug,
> with the scepter, and with their poles."

Reflection: When might we have directed our appreciation for something God provided to the wrong source?

Roughly one billion people in our world today lack access to clean, drinkable water. The rest of us seldom give water a thought. What can we do to thank Yahweh for his life-giving water? What can we do to help those who are thirsty?

May we give water to thirsty people in Jesus's name (Matthew 10:42).

[Check out Living Water International: https://water.cc/ for tangible ways to help.]

Psalm 155:

A Song of Victory

Numbers 21:27–30

As God's people travel through the desert and prepare to take the promised land, they come to the border of the Amorites. They ask King Sihon for permission to travel through the country, promising to stay on the main thoroughfare and not take any of the Amorites' food or water on the way.

Though this seems like a reasonable request, Sihon refuses. Instead, he rallies his army and attacks the people of Israel as they wait in the desert. The Israelites defend themselves, and they prevail. They take the land of the Amorites, along with the city of Heshbon, which King Sihon had captured from Moab.

Though the Israelites sought to peacefully travel through the Amorite territory, the king responded negatively, and he started a war. As a result, Israel defeated the Amorite army and took over their land.

In the aftermath of the battle, they sing a song of victory.

"Come to Heshbon.
  Let the city of Sihon be built and established;
for a fire has gone out of Heshbon,
  a flame from the city of Sihon.
It has devoured Ar of Moab,
  The lords of the high places of the Arnon.
Woe to you, Moab!
  You are undone, people of Chemosh!
He has given his sons as fugitives,
  and his daughters into captivity,
  to Sihon king of the Amorites.
We have shot at them.
  Heshbon has perished even to Dibon.
We have laid waste even to Nophah,
  Which reaches to Medeba."

Reflection: Though this passage may seem like mere gloating over a military conquest, remember that the Israelites sought a peaceful solution, and the Amorites attacked *them*. This is a song of deliverance from their enemies.

Though our enemy may not be an attacking army, we all have those who oppose us. We can trust that God will deliver us.

Have we ever sought an honorable solution to a problem and been wrongly attacked anyway? Did we ask God for his intervention? Did we praise him for his answer to our prayers?

May the Holy Spirit guide us to peaceful solutions whenever possible and protect us when peace with others eludes us.

Psalm 156:

An Interactive Liturgy

Deuteronomy 27:15–26

With the people poised to take the promised land, Moses recaps their forty-year history in the desert and reviews the instructions God gave them. At one point Moses leads the people in a liturgy of blessings (for obedience) and curses (for disobedience).

In this the Levites make a statement and the people respond in unison by saying "amen." In doing so they give their agreement to what the Levites say, a format similar to Psalm 136.

Interestingly, the Bible doesn't record the blessing portion of this liturgy, only the curses. This liturgy contains twelve statements of what the people should not do, actions for which they will receive a curse.

Here are Moses's instructions for this interactive liturgy:

"'Cursed is the man who makes an engraved or molten image, an abomination to Yahweh, the work of the hands of the craftsman, and sets it up in secret.'
All the people shall answer and say, 'Amen.'

'Cursed is he who dishonors his father or his mother.'
All the people shall say, 'Amen.'

'Cursed is he who removes his neighbor's landmark.'
All the people shall say, 'Amen.'

'Cursed is he who leads the blind astray on the road.'
All the people shall say, 'Amen.'

'Cursed is he who withholds justice from the foreigner, fatherless, and widow.'
All the people shall say, 'Amen.'

'Cursed is he who lies with his father's wife, because he dishonors his father's bed.'
All the people shall say, 'Amen.'

'Cursed is he who lies with any kind of animal.'
All the people shall say, 'Amen.'

'Cursed is he who lies with his sister, his father's daughter or his mother's daughter.'
All the people shall say, 'Amen.'

'Cursed is he who lies with his mother-in-law.'
All the people shall say, 'Amen.'

'Cursed is he who secretly kills his neighbor.'
All the people shall say, 'Amen.'

'Cursed is he who takes a bribe to kill an innocent person.'
All the people shall say, 'Amen.'

'Cursed is he who doesn't uphold the words of this law by doing them.'
All the people shall say, 'Amen.'"

Reflection: When we read Yahweh's commands in the Bible, do we respond with a hearty amen or dismiss them as instructions that no longer apply in our world today?

Though these curses relate to the Old Testament law, which Jesus fulfilled, does that mean we can disregard them? How might we apply these principles to our life and culture today?

May we respond with a sincere amen to whatever God says.

Psalm 157:

Moses's Final Song

Deuteronomy 32:1–43

Despite forty years of faithful service leading God's chosen people, God prohibits Moses from entering the promised land. This is all because of a single act of disobedience. This one action is enough to keep Moses from realizing the reward he desires.

It's a reminder that, through the law, one sin is enough to separate us from eternity with God. Fortunately, we're no longer under the law of Moses and can receive mercy through Jesus for eternity.

Regardless of the situation that Moses's action caused, he still maintains his focus on and reverence for God. With Moses's life winding down, he shares this song with the people and leaves them with a spiritual legacy.

Give ear, you heavens, and I will speak.
Let the earth hear the words of my mouth.
My doctrine will drop as the rain.
My speech will condense as the dew,
as the misty rain on the tender grass,
as the showers on the herb.
For I will proclaim Yahweh's name.
Ascribe greatness to our God!
The Rock: his work is perfect,
for all his ways are just.
A God of faithfulness who does no wrong,
just and right is he.
They have dealt corruptly with him.
They are not his children, because of their defect.
They are a perverse and crooked generation.
Is this the way you repay Yahweh,
foolish and unwise people?
Isn't he your father who has bought you?
He has made you and established you.
Remember the days of old.
Consider the years of many generations.
Ask your father, and he will show you;
your elders, and they will tell you.
When the Most High gave to the nations their inheritance,
when he separated the children of men,

he set the bounds of the peoples
   according to the number of the children of Israel.
For Yahweh's portion is his people.
   Jacob is the lot of his inheritance.
He found him in a desert land,
   in the waste howling wilderness.
He surrounded him.
   He cared for him.
   He kept him as the apple of his eye.
As an eagle that stirs up her nest,
   that flutters over her young,
he spread abroad his wings,
   he took them,
   he bore them on his feathers.
Yahweh alone led him.
   There was no foreign god with him.
He made him ride on the high places of the earth.
   He ate the increase of the field.
He caused him to suck honey out of the rock,
   oil out of the flinty rock;
butter from the herd, and milk from the flock,
   with fat of lambs,
   rams of the breed of Bashan, and goats,
   with the finest of the wheat.
   From the blood of the grape, you drank wine.
But Jeshurun grew fat, and kicked.
   You have grown fat.

You have grown thick.
You have become sleek.
Then he abandoned God who made him,
and rejected the Rock of his salvation.
They moved him to jealousy with strange gods.
They provoked him to anger with abominations.
They sacrificed to demons, not God,
to gods that they didn't know,
to new gods that came up recently,
which your fathers didn't dread.
Of the Rock who became your father, you are unmindful,
and have forgotten God who gave you birth.
Yahweh saw and abhorred,
because of the provocation of his sons and his daughters.
He said, "I will hide my face from them.
I will see what their end will be;
for they are a very perverse generation,
children in whom is no faithfulness.
They have moved me to jealousy with that which is not God.
They have provoked me to anger with their vanities.
I will move them to jealousy with those who are not a people.
I will provoke them to anger with a foolish nation.
For a fire is kindled in my anger,

that burns to the lowest Sheol,
devours the earth with its increase,
and sets the foundations of the mountains on fire.

"I will heap evils on them.
I will spend my arrows on them.
They shall be wasted with hunger,
and devoured with burning heat
and bitter destruction.
I will send the teeth of animals on them,
with the venom of vipers that glide in the dust.
Outside the sword will bereave,
and in the rooms,
terror on both young man and virgin,
the nursing infant with the gray-haired man.
I said that I would scatter them afar.
I would make their memory to cease from among men;
were it not that I feared the provocation of the enemy,
lest their adversaries should judge wrongly,
lest they should say, 'Our hand is exalted,
Yahweh has not done all this.'"

For they are a nation void of counsel.
There is no understanding in them.

Oh that they were wise, that they understood this,
that they would consider their latter end!
How could one chase a thousand,
and two put ten thousand to flight,
unless their Rock had sold them,
and Yahweh had delivered them up?
For their rock is not as our Rock,
even our enemies themselves concede.
For their vine is of the vine of Sodom,
of the fields of Gomorrah.
Their grapes are poison grapes.
Their clusters are bitter.
Their wine is the poison of serpents,
the cruel venom of asps.

"Isn't this laid up in store with me,
sealed up among my treasures?
Vengeance is mine, and recompense,
at the time when their foot slides;
for the day of their calamity is at hand.
Their doom rushes at them."

For Yahweh will judge his people,
and have compassion on his servants,
when he sees that their power is gone;
that there is no one remaining, shut up or left at large.

He will say, “Where are their gods,
  the rock in which they took refuge;
which ate the fat of their sacrifices,
  and drank the wine of their drink offering?
Let them rise up and help you!
  Let them be your protection.

“See now that I myself am he.
  There is no god with me.
I kill and I make alive.
  I wound and I heal.
  There is no one who can deliver out of my hand.
For I lift up my hand to heaven and declare,
  as I live forever,
if I sharpen my glittering sword,
  my hand grasps it in judgment;
I will take vengeance on my adversaries,
  and will repay those who hate me.
I will make my arrows drunk with blood.
  My sword shall devour flesh with the blood of the slain and the captives,
  from the head of the leaders of the enemy.”

Rejoice, you nations, with his people,
  for he will avenge the blood of his servants.
  He will take vengeance on his adversaries,

and will make atonement for his land and for his people.

Reflection: We are all moving through life toward the end of our physical existence.

As our life winds down, will our words overflow with hope or be driven by despair? What legacy will we leave behind, be it in written form or through the witness of a life lived well?

May we finish strong.

Psalm 158:

Moses's Parting Blessing

Deuteronomy 33:2–5

After Moses's final song he gives a blessing to the people. The first four verses of this passage read like a psalm. He then directs the rest of his oration to various tribes, much like a patriarch giving his final words to his children.

In the opening to his blessing, Moses refers to himself in the third person. It's as if he sees himself as already dead, offering these words from the grave.

"Yahweh came from Sinai,
  and rose from Seir to them.
He shone from Mount Paran.
  He came from the ten thousands of holy ones.
  At his right hand was a fiery law for them.
Yes, he loves the people.
  All his saints are in your hand.
  They sat down at your feet.

Each receives your words.
Moses commanded us a law,
an inheritance for the assembly of Jacob.
He was king in Jeshurun,
when the heads of the people were gathered,
all the tribes of Israel together."

Reflection: We should consider the legacy we will leave.

What will our final words be to our family and friends? How can we influence future generations after we're gone?

May we make our final words count.

Psalm 159:

Deborah's Song

Judges 5:2–31

After Moses dies, his successor, Joshua, leads the people to conquer and settle in the promised land. Then a series of judges (leaders) work to free the people from recurring cycles of oppression.

The book of Judges lists one female judge among many male counterparts. Deborah, a judge and a prophet, takes the mantle of leadership when Barak lacks the courage to do so by himself. Through her direction, God provides the nation of Israel with victory. In doing so, another woman, Jael, plays a decisive part.

Deborah (along with Barak) then offers this psalm of praise to God for delivering them from their enemies.

"Because the leaders took the lead in Israel,
because the people offered themselves willingly,
be blessed, Yahweh!

"Hear, you kings!
Give ear, you princes!
I, even I, will sing to Yahweh.
I will sing praise to Yahweh, the God of Israel.

"Yahweh, when you went out of Seir,
when you marched out of the field of Edom,
the earth trembled, the sky also dropped.
Yes, the clouds dropped water.
The mountains quaked at Yahweh's presence,
even Sinai at the presence of Yahweh, the God of Israel.

"In the days of Shamgar the son of Anath,
in the days of Jael, the highways were unoccupied.
The travelers walked through byways.
The rulers ceased in Israel.
They ceased until I, Deborah, arose;
Until I arose a mother in Israel.
They chose new gods.
Then war was in the gates.
Was there a shield or spear seen among forty thousand in Israel?
My heart is toward the governors of Israel,
who offered themselves willingly among the people.
Bless Yahweh!

"Speak, you who ride on white donkeys,
you who sit on rich carpets,
and you who walk by the way.
Far from the noise of archers, in the places of drawing water,
there they will rehearse Yahweh's righteous acts,
the righteous acts of his rule in Israel.

"Then Yahweh's people went down to the gates.
'Awake, awake, Deborah!
Awake, awake, utter a song!
Arise, Barak, and lead away your captives, you son of Abinoam.'

"Then a remnant of the nobles and the people came down.
Yahweh came down for me against the mighty.
Those whose root is in Amalek came out of Ephraim,
after you, Benjamin, among your peoples.
Governors come down out of Machir.
Those who handle the marshal's staff came out of Zebulun.
The princes of Issachar were with Deborah.
As was Issachar, so was Barak.
They rushed into the valley at his feet.

By the watercourses of Reuben,
   there were great resolves of heart.
Why did you sit among the sheepfolds?
   To hear the whistling for the flocks?
At the watercourses of Reuben,
   there were great searchings of heart.
Gilead lived beyond the Jordan.
   Why did Dan remain in ships?
   Asher sat still at the haven of the sea,
   and lived by his creeks.
Zebulun was a people that jeopardized their lives to the death;
   Naphtali also, on the high places of the field.

"The kings came and fought,
   then the kings of Canaan fought at Taanach by the waters of Megiddo.
   They took no plunder of silver.
From the sky the stars fought.
   From their courses, they fought against Sisera.
The river Kishon swept them away,
   that ancient river, the river Kishon.
   My soul, march on with strength.
Then the horse hoofs stamped because of the prancing,
   the prancing of their strong ones.
'Curse Meroz,' said Yahweh's angel.
   'Curse bitterly its inhabitants,

because they didn't come to help Yahweh,
to help Yahweh against the mighty.'

"Jael shall be blessed above women,
the wife of Heber the Kenite;
blessed shall she be above women in the tent.
He asked for water.
She gave him milk.
She brought him butter in a lordly dish.
She put her hand to the tent peg,
and her right hand to the workmen's hammer.
With the hammer she struck Sisera.
She struck through his head.
Yes, she pierced and struck through his temples.
At her feet he bowed, he fell, he lay.
At her feet he bowed, he fell.
Where he bowed, there he fell down dead.

"Through the window she looked out, and cried:
Sisera's mother looked through the lattice.
'Why is his chariot so long in coming?
Why do the wheels of his chariots wait?'
Her wise ladies answered her,
Yes, she returned answer to herself,
'Have they not found, have they not divided the plunder?
A lady, two ladies to every man;
to Sisera a plunder of dyed garments,

a plunder of dyed garments embroidered,
of dyed garments embroidered on both sides,
on the necks of the plunder?'

"So let all your enemies perish, Yahweh,
but let those who love him be as the sun when
it rises in its strength."

Reflection: Like Deborah, we may find ourselves in positions we didn't want. And like Barak, we may cower from what God wants us to do.

When faced with what we don't want, do we pull back in human fear or move forward in godly power? Are we able to praise Yahweh for the results?

May we have the courage to do what's right and what God calls us to do.

Psalm 160:

God's Provision

Ruth 4:14–15

Poor, widowed, and struggling to survive, Ruth lives with her destitute mother-in-law, Naomi. Yet God provides for Ruth (and her mother-in-law too) when Boaz marries Ruth as her kinsman-redeemer. Ruth and Boaz have a son—Ruth's first child and Naomi's first grandchild. (This boy, Obed, is the grandfather of the shepherd boy, David, who will one day become king over the nation of Israel.)

The women of the village share this psalm of praise with Ruth for God's marvelous provision.

> "Blessed be Yahweh, who has not left you today without a near kinsman. Let his name be famous in Israel. He shall be to you a restorer of life and sustain you in your old age; for your daughter-in-law, who loves you, who is better to you than seven sons, has given birth to him."

Reflection: The women praised Yahweh for providing Ruth with a husband and a son. Though most had families of their own, some of these women may have been waiting for a husband or longing for a child of their own, yet they celebrated with Ruth and Naomi anyway.

It's one thing to remember to praise God for his blessings to us, but do we think to praise him for his blessings to others?

May we thank God for the goodness other people receive from the Almighty.

Psalm 161:

Hannah's Prayer of Praise

1 Samuel 2:1–10

Hannah lives a difficult life. First, she must share her husband's affections with another woman. Second, Hannah is childless, while her husband's other wife, Peninnah, isn't. And Peninnah repeatedly mocks Hannah for her infertility.

Despite his love for her, Hannah's husband dismisses her pain over being childless. He doesn't understand her emotional anguish. At the temple Hannah prays earnestly for a son. But the priest accuses her of being drunk.

No one understands her, but God does. He hears her prayer and gives her a son, Samuel.

Here's Hannah's psalm of praise to God after the birth of her son.

"My heart exults in Yahweh!
My horn is exalted in Yahweh.
My mouth is enlarged over my enemies,
because I rejoice in your salvation.
There is no one as holy as Yahweh,
for there is no one besides you,
nor is there any rock like our God.

"Don't keep talking so exceedingly proudly.
Don't let arrogance come out of your mouth,
for Yahweh is a God of knowledge.
By him actions are weighed.

"The bows of the mighty men are broken.
Those who stumbled are armed with strength.
Those who were full have hired themselves out for bread.
Those who were hungry are satisfied.
Yes, the barren has borne seven.
She who has many children languishes.

"Yahweh kills and makes alive.
He brings down to Sheol and brings up.
Yahweh makes poor and makes rich.
He brings low, he also lifts up.
He raises up the poor out of the dust.
He lifts up the needy from the dunghill

to make them sit with princes
and inherit the throne of glory.
For the pillars of the earth are Yahweh's.
He has set the world on them.
He will keep the feet of his holy ones,
but the wicked will be put to silence in darkness;
for no man will prevail by strength.
Those who strive with Yahweh shall be broken to pieces.
He will thunder against them in the sky.

"Yahweh will judge the ends of the earth.
He will give strength to his king,
and exalt the horn of his anointed."

Reflection: There's no guarantee our life will turn out as we wish. And even when it seems everyone is against us, we can take comfort, knowing that God is always with us and will provide.

Do we praise God for his provisions? Are we willing to praise him during our discouraging times too?

May we offer our praise to Yahweh during the good times and the not-so-good times.

Psalm 162:

David's Lament for Saul and Jonathan

2 Samuel 1:19–27

Though Samuel has already anointed David as king, Saul continues to rule. David could move to seize the throne, but instead he patiently waits for God's timing. As he does, he respects Saul's authority as the reigning king. David also forms a tight bond with Saul's son Jonathan.

When Saul and Jonathan die in battle, the path is clear for David to ascend to the throne that God intended for him. David has every right to rejoice in Saul's death, since Saul tried to kill him multiple times. But David instead mourns Saul and Jonathan's passing.

"Your glory, Israel, was slain on your high places!
   How the mighty have fallen!
Don't tell it in Gath.

Don't publish it in the streets of Ashkelon,
lest the daughters of the Philistines rejoice,
lest the daughters of the uncircumcised triumph.
You mountains of Gilboa,
let there be no dew or rain on you, and no fields of offerings;
For there the shield of the mighty was defiled and cast away,
The shield of Saul was not anointed with oil.
From the blood of the slain,
from the fat of the mighty,
Jonathan's bow didn't turn back.
Saul's sword didn't return empty.
Saul and Jonathan were lovely and pleasant in their lives.
In their death, they were not divided.
They were swifter than eagles.
They were stronger than lions.
You daughters of Israel, weep over Saul,
who clothed you delicately in scarlet,
who put ornaments of gold on your clothing.
How the mighty have fallen in the middle of the battle!
Jonathan was slain on your high places.
I am distressed for you, my brother Jonathan.
You have been very pleasant to me.

Your love to me was wonderful,
passing the love of women.
How the mighty have fallen,
and the weapons of war have perished!"

Reflection: Like David when hearing of King Saul's death, we often have two ways to respond to the misfortunes of those who oppose us. We can be happy or sad. We can celebrate or grieve.

How do we respond when something good happens to us at the expense of another, such as the suffering of an enemy? How content are we to wait for God's perfect timing?

May we react to all situations in a God-honoring way.

Psalm 163:

David Mourns Abner's Death

2 Samuel 3:33–34

Abner is captain of Saul's army and initially opposes David. Later, he switches his allegiance. Nevertheless, Joab, the leader of David's army, kills Abner to avenge his brother's death.

David weeps for Abner and sings this lament.

> "Should Abner die as a fool dies? Your hands weren't bound, and your feet weren't put into fetters. As a man falls before the children of iniquity, so you fell."

Reflection: David viewed Abner's life as valuable. Joab didn't. David forgave. Joab held a grudge.

Do we value the lives of others? What can we do to elevate the lives of all people, regardless of their situation?

May we see others as God sees them.

Psalm 164:

David Praises God

1 Chronicles 16:8–36

After a fatal first attempt to move the ark of God (1 Chronicles 13:3–14), David successfully brings the ark of God into Jerusalem and places it inside the tent he has prepared for it. David then gives offerings to God and appoints Levites—including Asaph— to lead worship.

The Bible credits Asaph with twelve chapters in the book of Psalms. This may be his thirteenth one, though David could also have penned it.

Regardless of the authorship, here is this psalm to celebrate the arrival of the ark of the covenant.

Oh give thanks to Yahweh.
  Call on his name.
    Make what he has done known among the peoples.
Sing to him.

Sing praises to him.
Tell of all his marvelous works.
Glory in his holy name.
Let the heart of those who seek Yahweh rejoice.
Seek Yahweh and his strength.
Seek his face forever more.
Remember his marvelous works that he has done,
his wonders, and the judgments of his mouth,
you offspring of Israel his servant,
you children of Jacob, his chosen ones.
He is Yahweh our God.
His judgments are in all the earth.
Remember his covenant forever,
the word which he commanded to a thousand generations,
the covenant which he made with Abraham,
his oath to Isaac.
He confirmed it to Jacob for a statute,
and to Israel for an everlasting covenant,
saying, "I will give you the land of Canaan,
The lot of your inheritance,"
when you were but a few men in number,
yes, very few, and foreigners in it.
They went about from nation to nation,
from one kingdom to another people.
He allowed no man to do them wrong.

Yes, he reproved kings for their sakes,
"Don't touch my anointed ones!
Do my prophets no harm!"
Sing to Yahweh, all the earth!
Display his salvation from day to day.
Declare his glory among the nations,
and his marvelous works among all the peoples.
For great is Yahweh, and greatly to be praised.
He also is to be feared above all gods.
For all the gods of the peoples are idols,
but Yahweh made the heavens.
Honor and majesty are before him.
Strength and gladness are in his place.
Ascribe to Yahweh, you relatives of the peoples,
ascribe to Yahweh glory and strength!
Ascribe to Yahweh the glory due to his name.
Bring an offering, and come before him.
Worship Yahweh in holy array.
Tremble before him, all the earth.
The world also is established that it can't be moved.
Let the heavens be glad,
and let the earth rejoice!
Let them say among the nations, "Yahweh reigns!"
Let the sea roar, and its fullness!
Let the field exult, and all that is in it!

Then the trees of the forest will sing for joy before
    Yahweh,
  for he comes to judge the earth.
Oh give thanks to Yahweh, for he is good,
  for his loving kindness endures forever.
Say, "Save us, God of our salvation!
    Gather us together and deliver us from the
    nations,
  to give thanks to your holy name,
  to triumph in your praise."
Blessed be Yahweh, the God of Israel,
  from everlasting even to everlasting.

Reflection: It's human nature to want to receive credit for what we have done. Though we're not sure who wrote this psalm—David or Asaph—the author is not the issue. The point is worshiping Yahweh, and this psalm does a superb job at it.

When have we strived to receive recognition for our work and in the process distracted others from worshiping God? Are we willing to set aside our pride so that others can best connect with the Almighty?

As John the Baptist said about Jesus, "He must increase, but I must decrease" (John 3:30). May we adopt the same humble perspective.

Psalm 165:

David's Song of Praise

2 Samuel 7:18–29

King David secures his throne, and the Almighty blesses him with peace. David desires to build a temple for Yahweh. At first the prophet Nathan agrees, but that night God reveals his perspective to his spokesman. David is not to build the temple because he is a warrior and has shed blood (1 Chronicles 28:3). Instead, the task will fall to one of David's descendants.

Nathan reveals God's instructions to David, and the king accepts the prophet's disappointing words. David sits before God and prays this psalm to the Almighty.

This psalm (similar to 1 Chronicles 17:16–27) appears in paragraph form and lacks the stanza formatting we're used to seeing in the book of Psalms. Nevertheless, the text still reads like a psalm.

> "Who am I, Lord Yahweh, and what is my house, that you have brought me this far? This was yet a

small thing in your eyes, Lord Yahweh; but you have spoken also of your servant's house for a great while to come; and this among men, Lord Yahweh! What more can David say to you? For you know your servant, Lord Yahweh. For your word's sake, and according to your own heart, you have worked all this greatness, to make your servant know it. Therefore you are great, Yahweh God. For there is no one like you, neither is there any God besides you, according to all that we have heard with our ears. What one nation in the earth is like your people, even like Israel, whom God went to redeem to himself for a people, and to make himself a name, and to do great things for you, and awesome things for your land, before your people, whom you redeemed to yourself out of Egypt, from the nations and their gods? You established for yourself your people Israel to be your people forever; and you, Yahweh, became their God. Now, Yahweh God, the word that you have spoken concerning your servant, and concerning his house, confirm it forever, and do as you have spoken. Let your name be magnified forever, saying, 'Yahweh of Armies is God over Israel; and the house of your servant David will be established before you.' For you, Yahweh of Armies, the God of Israel, have

> revealed to your servant, saying, 'I will build you a house.' Therefore your servant has found in his heart to pray this prayer to you.
>
> "Now, O Lord Yahweh, you are God, and your words are truth, and you have promised this good thing to your servant. Now therefore let it please you to bless the house of your servant, that it may continue forever before you; for you, Lord Yahweh, have spoken it. Let the house of your servant be blessed forever with your blessing."

Reflection: David was surely disappointed when God prohibited him from building a temple. Yet instead of being upset and responding bitterly, David instead praises Yahweh for his provisions and asks for continued favor.

How do we respond to disappointment? Do we complain to the Almighty or see the good that he has done and praise him for his character?

May our character reflect our Creator's.

Psalm 166:

David Affirms God

1 Chronicles 29:10–19

After God tells David—through Nathan—that he is not the one to build God's temple, David collects materials for its future construction. In addition to his own resources, other leaders also give willingly toward the temple's construction.

In this the people and David rejoice. Here's what David says.

> "You are blessed, Yahweh, the God of Israel our father, forever and ever. Yours, Yahweh, is the greatness, the power, the glory, the victory, and the majesty! For all that is in the heavens and in the earth is yours. Yours is the kingdom, Yahweh, and you are exalted as head above all. Both riches and honor come from you, and you rule over all! In your hand is power and might! It is in your hand to make great, and to give strength to

all! Now therefore, our God, we thank you, and praise your glorious name. But who am I, and what is my people, that we should be able to offer so willingly as this? For all things come from you, and we have given you of your own. For we are strangers before you, and foreigners, as all our fathers were. Our days on the earth are as a shadow, and there is no remaining. Yahweh our God, all this store that we have prepared to build you a house for your holy name comes from your hand, and is all your own. I know also, my God, that you try the heart, and have pleasure in uprightness. As for me, in the uprightness of my heart I have willingly offered all these things. Now I have seen with joy your people, who are present here, offer willingly to you. Yahweh, the God of Abraham, of Isaac, and of Israel, our fathers, keep this desire forever in the thoughts of the heart of your people, and prepare their heart for you; and give to Solomon my son a perfect heart, to keep your commandments, your testimonies, and your statutes, and to do all these things, and to build the palace, for which I have made provision."

Reflection: This example of people who give willingly, generously, and with joy delights David and surely delights Yahweh. Much later, the apostle Paul tells the church in Corinth that God loves those who give cheerfully (2 Corinthians 9:7).

Do we give like the people in David's day: willingly, generously, and with joy? Do we align with Paul's encouragement to give cheerfully?

May we give to God and his causes with motives that lift our spirits and delight him.

Psalm 167:

David Worships God for Deliverance

2 Samuel 22:2–51

Second Samuel 22 looks back at one of the times when God delivered David from King Saul's attempt to kill him. If this scenario sounds familiar and this passage from 2 Samuel looks just like a Psalm, you are correct.

This song of praise from 2 Samuel 22 is quite similar to Psalm 18. Many verses are an exact match, while others contain parallel thoughts. It's as if one passage is a first draft and the other, a final version. But if so, we can only speculate which one came first.

Here is the version of David's psalm of praise as recorded in 2 Samuel 22.

"Yahweh is my rock,
my fortress,
and my deliverer, even mine;

God is my rock in whom I take refuge;
my shield, and the horn of my salvation,
my high tower, and my refuge.
My savior, you save me from violence.
I call on Yahweh, who is worthy to be praised;
So shall I be saved from my enemies.
For the waves of death surrounded me.
The floods of ungodliness made me afraid.
The cords of Sheol were around me.
The snares of death caught me.
In my distress, I called on Yahweh.
Yes, I called to my God.
He heard my voice out of his temple.
My cry came into his ears.
Then the earth shook and trembled.
The foundations of heaven quaked and were shaken,
because he was angry.
Smoke went up out of his nostrils.
Consuming fire came out of his mouth.
Coals were kindled by it.
He bowed the heavens also, and came down.
Thick darkness was under his feet.
He rode on a cherub, and flew.
Yes, he was seen on the wings of the wind.
He made darkness a shelter around himself:
gathering of waters, and thick clouds of the skies.
At the brightness before him,
coals of fire were kindled.

Yahweh thundered from heaven.
The Most High uttered his voice.
He sent out arrows and scattered them,
lightning and confused them.
Then the channels of the sea appeared.
The foundations of the world were laid bare by Yahweh's rebuke,
at the blast of the breath of his nostrils.
He sent from on high and he took me.
He drew me out of many waters.
He delivered me from my strong enemy,
from those who hated me, for they were too mighty for me.
They came on me in the day of my calamity,
but Yahweh was my support.
He also brought me out into a large place.
He delivered me, because he delighted in me.
Yahweh rewarded me according to my righteousness.
He rewarded me according to the cleanness of my hands.
For I have kept Yahweh's ways,
and have not wickedly departed from my God.
For all his ordinances were before me.
As for his statutes, I didn't depart from them.
I was also perfect toward him.
I kept myself from my iniquity.
Therefore Yahweh has rewarded me according to my righteousness,

According to my cleanness in his eyesight.
With the merciful you will show yourself merciful.
With the perfect man you will show yourself perfect.
With the pure you will show yourself pure.
With the crooked you will show yourself shrewd.
You will save the afflicted people,
But your eyes are on the arrogant, that you may bring them down.
For you are my lamp, Yahweh.
Yahweh will light up my darkness.
For by you, I run against a troop.
By my God, I leap over a wall.
As for God, his way is perfect.
Yahweh's word is tested.
He is a shield to all those who take refuge in him.
For who is God, besides Yahweh?
Who is a rock, besides our God?
God is my strong fortress.
He makes my way perfect.
He makes his feet like hinds' feet,
and sets me on my high places.
He teaches my hands to war,
so that my arms bend a bow of bronze.
You have also given me the shield of your salvation.
Your gentleness has made me great.
You have enlarged my steps under me.
My feet have not slipped.

I have pursued my enemies and destroyed them.
I didn't turn again until they were consumed.
I have consumed them,
and struck them through,
so that they can't arise.
Yes, they have fallen under my feet.
For you have armed me with strength for the battle.
You have subdued under me those who rose up against me.
You have also made my enemies turn their backs to me,
that I might cut off those who hate me.
They looked, but there was no one to save;
even to Yahweh, but he didn't answer them.
Then I beat them as small as the dust of the earth.
I crushed them as the mire of the streets, and spread them abroad.
You also have delivered me from the strivings of my people.
You have kept me to be the head of the nations.
A people whom I have not known will serve me.
The foreigners will submit themselves to me.
As soon as they hear of me, they will obey me.
The foreigners will fade away,
and will come trembling out of their close places.
Yahweh lives!

Blessed be my rock!
Exalted be God, the rock of my salvation,
even the God who executes vengeance for me,
who brings down peoples under me,
who brings me away from my enemies.
Yes, you lift me up above those who rise up against me.
You deliver me from the violent man.
Therefore I will give thanks to you, Yahweh, among the nations,
and will sing praises to your name.
He gives great deliverance to his king,
and shows loving kindness to his anointed,
to David and to his offspring, forever more."

Reflection: The placement of this psalm in 2 Samuel seems out of chronological order. Though the event immortalized by this psalm happened earlier in David's life, it might not be until much later that he writes his words of appreciation to Yahweh. But it doesn't really matter *when* David wrote his song of praise to God, only that he did.

Thinking back on our lives, when have we forgotten to thank the Almighty for his provisions, for his blessings? It's not too late. Praise him now. Do it in prayer, in song, or in a psalm of your own.

May we remember to praise Yahweh.

Psalm 168:

David's Last Words

2 Samuel 23:2–7

As the book of 2 Samuel winds down, so does David's life. In the penultimate chapter, we read David's final recorded words. In this short psalm of praise, David recites the words God spoke to him, affirming David's godly character and righteous reign.

"Yahweh's Spirit spoke by me.
  His word was on my tongue.
The God of Israel said,
  the Rock of Israel spoke to me,
  'One who rules over men righteously,
  who rules in the fear of God,
shall be as the light of the morning, when the
    sun rises,
  a morning without clouds,
  when the tender grass springs out of the earth,

through clear shining after rain.'
Isn't my house so with God?
Yet he has made with me an everlasting covenant,
ordered in all things, and sure,
for it is all my salvation and all my desire,
although he doesn't make it grow.
But all the ungodly will be as thorns to be thrust away,
because they can't be taken with the hand.
The man who touches them must be armed with iron and the staff of a spear.
They will be utterly burned with fire in their place."

Reflection: The last words we say in our life here on earth may be recorded for others to read. In doing so, we can talk about ourselves, or we can talk about God. Or we can do both, reminding others of our relationship with the Almighty and the lifetime of blessings he provided.

What can we do to make sure our final words matter the most for those closest to us? Should we write them down so that future generations can read them and praise God?

May our last words celebrate Yahweh and point others to him.

Psalm 169:

King Hiram's Testimony

2 Chronicles 2:11–12

David's son Solomon replaces his father as king and prepares to build the temple for God. In addition to the materials David had already stockpiled, Solomon requests cedar logs, other resources, and a skilled artist from Hiram (Huram), king of Tyre.

King Hiram is pleased to assist and responds in a letter to King Solomon. His correspondence opens with his own psalm of praise to God.

> "Because Yahweh loves his people, he has made you king over them . . .
>
> "Blessed be Yahweh, the God of Israel, who made heaven and earth, who has given to David the king a wise son, endowed with discretion and understanding, who would build a house for Yahweh, and a house for his kingdom."

Reflection: We don't know about King Hiram's standing with Yahweh. Not being one of God's chosen people, it's easy to assume that Hiram doesn't have a relationship with the Almighty. Yet his words praise Yahweh as Creator. This may be a result of personal belief or his assumption based on what he witnessed in King David's life.

When we hear someone praise God or make a surprising declaration, do we dismiss it because they're not from our group? Or do we embrace their words and worship God without judging the source?

May we see others as God sees them and refrain from dismissing them.

Psalm 170:

Solomon Brings the Ark into the Temple

1 Kings 8:15–21

As successor to King David, Solomon constructs the temple that his father wanted to build. With much fanfare Solomon brings the ark—which contains the two stone tablets God gave to Moses—to reside in the temple.

Before the people gather for this momentous event, Solomon blesses God and honors David. (This passage repeats in 2 Chronicles 6:4–11, and we find Solomon's two other Psalms in Psalm 72 and 127.)

> "Blessed is Yahweh, the God of Israel, who spoke with his mouth to David your father, and has with his hand fulfilled it, saying, 'Since the day that I brought my people Israel out of Egypt, I chose no city out of all the tribes of Israel to build a house, that my name might be there; but I chose David to be over my people Israel.'

> "Now it was in the heart of David my father to build a house for the name of Yahweh, the God of Israel. But Yahweh said to David my father, 'Whereas it was in your heart to build a house for my name, you did well that it was in your heart. Nevertheless, you shall not build the house; but your son who shall come out of your body, he shall build the house for my name.' Yahweh has established his word that he spoke; for I have risen up in the place of David my father, and I sit on the throne of Israel, as Yahweh promised, and have built the house for the name of Yahweh, the God of Israel. There I have set a place for the ark, in which is Yahweh's covenant, which he made with our fathers, when he brought them out of the land of Egypt."

Reflection: This passage opens with a blessing to Yahweh, but then it shifts to give tribute to Solomon's father, King David. Solomon concludes by looking at what he accomplished. We could interpret this either as Solomon's ego poking through or as praise to God for what Yahweh accomplished through the king.

Has our praise to the Almighty ever come across as calling attention to what we did? Though we may give God credit in this, it's easy to wrongly elevate ourselves in the process.

May we rightly place our focus on Yahweh and what he has done.

Psalm 171:

Solomon Dedicates the Temple

1 Kings 8:23–53

After bringing the ark to the temple, Solomon stands before the altar, lifts his hands to heaven, and offers these words to God:

"Yahweh, the God of Israel, there is no God like you, in heaven above, or on earth beneath; who keeps covenant and loving kindness with your servants, who walk before you with all their heart; who has kept with your servant David my father that which you promised him. Yes, you spoke with your mouth, and have fulfilled it with your hand, as it is today. Now therefore, may Yahweh, the God of Israel, keep with your servant David my father that which you have promised him, saying, 'There shall not fail from you a man in my sight to sit on the throne of Israel, if only your children take heed to their way, to walk before me as you have walked before me.'

"Now therefore, God of Israel, please let your word be verified, which you spoke to your servant David my father. But will God in very deed dwell on the earth? Behold, heaven and the heaven of heavens can't contain you; how much less this house that I have built! Yet have respect for the prayer of your servant, and for his supplication, Yahweh my God, to listen to the cry and to the prayer which your servant prays before you today; that your eyes may be open toward this house night and day, even toward the place of which you have said, 'My name shall be there;' to listen to the prayer which your servant prays toward this place. Listen to the supplication of your servant, and of your people Israel, when they pray toward this place. Yes, hear in heaven, your dwelling place; and when you hear, forgive.

"If a man sins against his neighbor, and an oath is laid on him to cause him to swear, and he comes and swears before your altar in this house; then hear in heaven, and act, and judge your servants, condemning the wicked, to bring his way on his own head, and justifying the righteous, to give him according to his righteousness.

"When your people Israel are struck down before the enemy, because they have sinned against you; if they turn again to you, and confess your name, and pray and make supplication to you in this house; then hear in heaven, and forgive the sin of your people Israel, and bring them again to the land which you gave to their fathers.

"When the sky is shut up, and there is no rain, because they have sinned against you; if they pray toward this place, and confess your name, and turn from their sin, when you afflict them, then hear in heaven, and forgive the sin of your servants, and of your people Israel, when you teach them the good way in which they should walk; and send rain on your land, which you have given to your people for an inheritance.

"If there is famine in the land, if there is pestilence, if there is blight, mildew, locust or caterpillar; if their enemy besieges them in the land of their cities; whatever plague, whatever sickness there is; whatever prayer and supplication is made by any man, or by all your people Israel, who shall each know the plague of his own heart, and spread out his hands toward this house, then hear in heaven, your dwelling place, and forgive, and act, and give to every man according to all his ways, whose heart you know (for you, even you only, know the hearts of all the children of men); that they may fear you all the days that they live in the land which you gave to our fathers.

"Moreover concerning the foreigner, who is not of your people Israel, when he comes out of a far country for your name's sake (for they shall hear of your great name, and of your mighty hand, and of your outstretched arm); when he comes and prays toward this house; hear in heaven, your dwelling place, and do according to all that the foreigner calls to you for; that all the peoples of the earth may know your name, to fear you, as do your people Israel, and that they may know that this house which I have built is called by your name.

"If your people go out to battle against their enemy, by whatever way you shall send them, and they pray to Yahweh toward the city which you have chosen, and toward the house which I have built for your name; then hear in heaven their prayer and their supplication, and maintain their cause. If they sin against you (for there is no man who doesn't sin), and you are angry with them, and deliver them to the enemy, so that they carry them away captive to the land of the enemy, far off or near; yet if they repent in the land where they are carried captive, and turn again, and make supplication to you in the land of those who carried them captive, saying, 'We have sinned, and have done perversely; we have dealt wickedly;' if they return to you with all their heart and with all their soul in the land of their enemies, who carried them captive, and pray to you toward their land, which you gave to their fathers, the city which you have chosen, and the house which I have built for your name; then hear their prayer and their supplication in heaven, your dwelling place, and maintain their cause; and forgive your people who have sinned against you, and all their transgressions in which they have transgressed against you; and give them compassion before those who carried them captive, that they may have compassion on them (for they are your people, and your inheritance, which you brought out of Egypt, from the middle of the iron furnace); that your eyes may be open to the supplication of your servant,

> and to the supplication of your people Israel, to listen to them whenever they cry to you. For you separated them from among all the peoples of the earth, to be your inheritance, as you spoke by Moses your servant, when you brought our fathers out of Egypt, Lord Yahweh."

Reflection: Though the Bible doesn't call this oration a prayer, it sounds like one, interspersing praise with petition, along with some forward-looking portions that seem much like prophecy. This reminds us that our interaction with our Creator can take many forms and have intertwined formats.

When we approach Yahweh, do we focus on the eloquence of our words or come to him without pretense?

May our praise stem from a pure heart with a desire to connect with the Almighty.

Psalm 172:

Solomon's Blessing

1 Kings 8:56–61

After bringing the ark to the temple and dedicating it, the third part of this public ceremony is Solomon's blessing to God, which emerges as a psalm of praise to him and instruction to the people.

> "Blessed be Yahweh, who has given rest to his people Israel, according to all that he promised. There has not failed one word of all his good promise, which he promised by Moses his servant. May Yahweh our God be with us, as he was with our fathers. Let him not leave us or forsake us; that he may incline our hearts to him, to walk in all his ways, and to keep his commandments, and his statutes, and his ordinances, which he commanded our fathers. Let these my words, with which I have made supplication before Yahweh, be near to Yahweh

> our God day and night, that he may maintain the cause of his servant, and the cause of his people Israel, as every day requires; that all the peoples of the earth may know that Yahweh himself is God. There is no one else.
>
> "Let your heart therefore be perfect with Yahweh our God, to walk in his statutes, and to keep his commandments, as it is today."

Reflection: Serving as a fitting conclusion to Solomon's celebration of God's temple, this final passage wraps up with an encouragement to the people to turn their hearts to Yahweh, walk with him, and obey what he says.

How well do we do at attuning our hearts to Yahweh and obeying his commandments? How should we adjust our perspective or change our actions?

May all that we do and say align with God's will for us.

Psalm 173:

The People Praise God

2 Chronicles 5:13, 7:3, 20:21, and Ezra 3:11

It's hard for a large group of people to recite a long passage in unison, but they can do quite well with shorter phrases.

Three times in the book of 2 Chronicles and once in the book of Ezra, the people collectively praise God. Each time their succinct response rises as a psalm of adoration.

The first occurrence is when Solomon dedicates the temple (2 Chronicles 5:13). The second time is right after that when fire comes down from heaven and God's glory fills the temple (2 Chronicles 7:3). The third occurs much later when King Jehoshaphat appoints singers to lead the army (2 Chronicles 20:21).

The final time occurs even later still. Some people receive permission to return to their homeland after being conquered and exiled for their disobedience to God. They repair the altar and resume their sacrifices to God as prescribed by Moses. Then they work on rebuilding the temple. With the foundation laid, the people celebrate in song, with a great shout to God (Ezra 3:11).

Though the details and exact wording vary a bit, in each of these four examples, we can easily envision the people chanting (or singing) this psalm of praise over and over. Imagine their concise liturgy emerging as an escalating celebration of God.

> "For he is good;
>
> for his loving kindness endures forever!"

Reflection: To get a better idea of what this could sound like, consider Psalm 136, where the people's liturgical reaction is the similar recurring phrase, "for his loving kindness endures forever." In this Psalm the phrase repeats twenty-six times in response to various affirmations of who God is and what he does.

Are we willing to praise Yahweh aloud in corporate worship as good, whose loving kindness endures forever? If we hesitate to do so because it seems awkward or unfamiliar, does our attitude toward worship need to change?

May we sing and chant our adoration to Almighty God.

Psalm 174:

Jehoshaphat's Prayer

2 Chronicles 20:6–12

Several nations come to wage war against the nation of Judah. King Jehoshaphat declares a fast, and the people come together to seek God. Jehoshaphat stands before the people and says this prayer. It sounds much like a psalm seeking deliverance (such as Psalm 86 and many others).

> "Yahweh, the God of our fathers, aren't you God in heaven? Aren't you ruler over all the kingdoms of the nations? Power and might are in your hand, so that no one is able to withstand you. Didn't you, our God, drive out the inhabitants of this land before your people Israel, and give it to the offspring of Abraham your friend forever? They lived in it, and have built you a sanctuary in it for your name, saying, 'If evil comes on us—the sword, judgment, pestilence, or famine—we

> will stand before this house, and before you (for your name is in this house), and cry to you in our affliction, and you will hear and save.' Now, behold, the children of Ammon and Moab and Mount Seir, whom you would not let Israel invade when they came out of the land of Egypt, but they turned away from them, and didn't destroy them; behold, how they reward us, to come to cast us out of your possession, which you have given us to inherit. Our God, will you not judge them? For we have no might against this great company that comes against us. We don't know what to do, but our eyes are on you."

Reflection: With the enemy army approaching, the logical reaction is to gather the troops and mount a response. Yet Jehoshaphat doesn't do this. Instead, he tells the people to fast and gather. Then he prays.

When faced with a tangible threat, do we plan a human defense or first seek Yahweh? When confronted with opposition, do we fast and pray or fret and worry?

May we discern a God-honoring balance of when we should seek him and when we should move forward under his power.

Psalm 175:

A Historical Remembrance

Nehemiah 9:5–38

After a remnant of the exiled people return to the promise land, Ezra and Nehemiah continue to reform the people's spiritual practices. In response, the community separates themselves from foreigners and confesses their sins and the sins of their ancestors. Then they hear the law read to them.

In response to hearing God's Word, eight Levites tell the people to stand and praise their eternal God. What follows is a psalm that recaps the nation's interaction with Yahweh, smartly summarizing the entire Old Testament up to this point.

But this passage is more than a history lesson (like Psalm 106 and 136). This psalm opens with adoration of God and closes with the people making and sealing a covenant with God.

Here is the Levites' psalm of praise, remembrance, and petition.

"Stand up and bless Yahweh your God from everlasting to everlasting! Blessed be your glorious name, which is exalted above all blessing and praise! You are Yahweh, even you alone. You have made heaven, the heaven of heavens, with all their army, the earth and all things that are on it, the seas and all that is in them, and you preserve them all. The army of heaven worships you. You are Yahweh, the God who chose Abram, brought him out of Ur of the Chaldees, gave him the name of Abraham, found his heart faithful before you, and made a covenant with him to give the land of the Canaanite, the Hittite, the Amorite, the Perizzite, the Jebusite, and the Girgashite, to give it to his offspring, and have performed your words; for you are righteous.

"You saw the affliction of our fathers in Egypt, and heard their cry by the Red Sea, and showed signs and wonders against Pharaoh, and against all his servants, and against all the people of his land; for you knew that they dealt proudly against them, and made a name for yourself, as it is today. You divided the sea before them, so that they went through the middle of the sea on the dry land; and you cast their pursuers into the depths, as a stone into the mighty waters. Moreover, in a pillar of cloud you led them by day; and in a pillar of fire by night, to give them light in the way in which they should go.

"You also came down on Mount Sinai, and spoke with them from heaven, and gave them right ordinances and true laws, good statutes and commandments, and made known to them your holy Sabbath, and commanded them commandments, statutes, and a law, by Moses your servant, and gave them bread from the sky for their hunger, and brought water out of the rock for them for their thirst, and commanded them that they should go in to possess the land which you had sworn to give them.

"But they and our fathers behaved proudly, hardened their neck, didn't listen to your commandments, and refused to obey. They weren't mindful of your wonders that you did among them, but hardened their neck, and in their rebellion appointed a captain to return to their bondage. But you are a God ready to pardon, gracious and merciful, slow to anger, and abundant in loving kindness, and didn't forsake them. Yes, when they had made themselves a molded calf, and said, 'This is your God who brought you up out of Egypt,' and had committed awful blasphemies; yet you in your manifold mercies didn't forsake them in the wilderness. The pillar of cloud didn't depart from over them by day, to lead them in the way; neither did the pillar of fire by night, to show them light, and the way in which they should go. You gave also your good Spirit to instruct them, and didn't withhold your manna from their mouth, and gave them water for their thirst.

"Yes, forty years you sustained them in the wilderness. They lacked nothing. Their clothes didn't grow old, and their feet didn't swell. Moreover you gave them kingdoms and peoples, which you allotted according to their portions. So they possessed the land of Sihon, even the land of the king of Heshbon, and the land of Og king of Bashan. You also multiplied their children as the stars of the sky, and brought them into the land concerning which you said to their fathers, that they should go in to possess it.

"So the children went in and possessed the land, and you subdued before them the inhabitants of the land, the Canaanites, and gave them into their hands, with their kings and the peoples of the land, that they might do with them as they pleased. They took fortified cities and a rich land, and possessed houses full of all good things, cisterns dug out, vineyards, olive groves, and fruit trees in abundance. So they ate, were filled, became fat, and delighted themselves in your great goodness.

"Nevertheless they were disobedient, and rebelled against you, cast your law behind their back, killed your prophets that testified against them to turn them again to you, and they committed awful blasphemies. Therefore you delivered them into the hand of their adversaries, who distressed them. In the time of their trouble, when they cried to you, you heard from heaven; and according to your manifold mercies you gave them saviors who saved them out of the hands of their adversaries. But after they had rest, they did evil again before you; therefore you left them in the hands of their enemies, so that they had the dominion over them; yet when they returned, and cried to you, you heard from heaven; and many times you delivered them according to your mercies, and testified against them, that you might bring them again to your law. Yet they were arrogant, and didn't listen to your commandments, but sinned against your ordinances (which if a man does, he shall live in them), turned their backs, stiffened their neck, and would not hear. Yet many years you put up with them, and testified against them by your Spirit through your prophets. Yet they would not listen. Therefore you gave them into the hand of the peoples of the lands.

"Nevertheless in your manifold mercies you didn't make a full end of them, nor forsake them; for you are a gracious and merciful God.

Now therefore, our God, the great, the mighty, and the awesome God, who keeps covenant and loving kindness, don't let all the travail seem little before you, that has come on us, on our kings, on our princes, on our priests, on our prophets, on our fathers, and on all your people, since the time of the kings of Assyria to this day. However you are just in all that has come on us; for you

> have dealt truly, but we have done wickedly. Also our kings, our princes, our priests, and our fathers have not kept your law, nor listened to your commandments and your testimonies with which you testified against them. For they have not served you in their kingdom, and in your great goodness that you gave them, and in the large and rich land which you gave before them. They didn't turn from their wicked works.
>
> "Behold, we are servants today, and as for the land that you gave to our fathers to eat its fruit and its good, behold, we are servants in it. It yields much increase to the kings whom you have set over us because of our sins. Also they have power over our bodies and over our livestock, at their pleasure, and we are in great distress. Yet for all this, we make a sure covenant, and write it; and our princes, our Levites, and our priests, seal it."

Reflection: There's an astute saying that those who don't learn from history are doomed to repeat it. God's chosen people certainly exemplify this in their recurring cycles of obedience, disobedience, and punishment. If only they would learn from the mistakes of prior generations.

Yet their history also teaches us. Are we willing to consider their failings so that we may avoid them?

What about church history since the days of Jesus? We've made many mistakes over the ensuing two thousand years. Are we able to learn from them and avoid their errors? Or are we doomed to repeat the same missteps of our predecessors?

May we learn from the faults of all who've gone before us so that we don't repeat their failures.

Psalm 176:

Mordecai's Plea

Esther 4:19–27

There are two versions of the book of Esther. The shorter version, found in most—but not all—Protestant Bibles, is based on the traditional Hebrew text.

The expanded version of Esther, found in most other Bibles, contains five additional passages as found in the Septuagint, the collection of Scriptures commonly used in Jesus's day and which he quoted from.

If considering these additional passages from Esther disturbs you, skip over the next two chapters. Or continue reading to explore what you might learn about God from the Bible's other psalms.

After Mordecai learns of Haman's plan to exterminate the Jews, he communicates the plot to Esther, and they plan how to proceed. Mordecai will gather the Jews in the city to fast for three days. Then Esther will approach the king, though without an official summons she risks execution for disregarding protocols.

Mordecai then pleads with God in prayer and requests deliverance. Mordecai's prayer parallels Psalms 17, 86, 90, and 124.

> "Lord God, you are king ruling over all, for all things are in your power, and there is no one who can oppose you in your purpose to save Israel; for you have made the heaven and the earth and every wonderful thing under heaven. You are Lord of all, and there is no one who can resist you, Lord. You know all things. You know, Lord, that it is not in insolence, nor arrogance, nor love of glory, that I have done this, to refuse to bow down to the arrogant Haman. For I would gladly have kissed the soles of his feet for the safety of Israel. But I have done this that I might not set the glory of man above the glory of God. I will not worship anyone except you, my Lord, and I will not do these things in arrogance. And now, O Lord God, the King, the God of Abraham, spare your people, for our enemies are planning our destruction, and they have desired to destroy your ancient inheritance. Do not overlook your people, whom you have redeemed for yourself

> out of the land of Egypt. Listen to my prayer. Have mercy on your inheritance and turn our mourning into gladness, that we may live and sing praise to your name, O Lord. Don't utterly destroy the mouth of those who praise you, O Lord."

Reflection: Sometimes our role is to act, like Esther. Other times our place is to fast and pray, like Mordecai—and Esther as well. Sometimes seeking God is the *best* thing we can do. What we want to avoid, however, is acting on our own accord without seeking God first and moving under his power.

When have we acted first and prayed only after things fell apart? When have we prayed and then failed to act, even though we had the opportunity to do so?

When our role has been to pray, have we done so? Have we been content with that?

May we discern when to pray, when to act, and when to do both.

Psalm 177:

Esther's Petition

Esther 4:31–47

In addition to Mordecai's psalm-like prayer, the expanded version of the book of Esther also records Esther's psalm of petition. In it she humbles herself, confesses the sins of her people, and respectfully pleads for God's deliverance.

> "O my Lord, you alone are our king. Help me. I am destitute, and have no helper but you, for my danger is near at hand. I have heard from my birth in the tribe of my kindred that you, Lord, took Israel out of all the nations, and our fathers out of all their kindred for a perpetual inheritance, and have done for them all that you have said.

“And now we have sinned before you, and you have delivered us into the hands of our enemies, because we honored their gods. You are righteous, O Lord.

“But now they have not been content with the bitterness of our slavery, but have laid their hands on the hands of their idols to abolish the decree of your mouth, and utterly to destroy your inheritance, and to stop the mouth of those who praise you, and to extinguish the glory of your house and your altar, and to open the mouth of the Gentiles to speak the praises of vanities, and that a mortal king should be admired forever.

“O Lord, don’t surrender your sceptre to those who don’t exist, and don’t let them laugh at our fall, but turn their counsel against themselves, and make an example of him who has begun to injure us.

“Remember us, O Lord! Manifest yourself in the time of our affliction. Encourage me, O King of gods, and ruler of all dominion!

“Put harmonious speech into my mouth before the lion, and turn his heart to hate him who fights against us, to the utter destruction of those who agree with him.

“But deliver us by your hand, and help me who am alone and have no one but you, O Lord.

“You know all things, and know that I hate the glory of transgressors, and that I abhor the bed of the uncircumcised and of every stranger.

“You know my necessity, for I abhor the symbol of my proud station, which is upon my head in the days of my splendor. I abhor it as a menstruous cloth, and I don’t wear it in the days of my tranquility.

“Your handmaid has not eaten at Haman’s table, and I have not honored the banquet of the king, neither have I drunk wine of libations.

> "Neither has your handmaid rejoiced since the day of my promotion until now, except in you, O Lord God of Abraham.
>
> "O god, who has power over all, listen to the voice of the desperate, and deliver us from the hand of those who devise mischief. Deliver me from my fear."

Reflection: Again, we see the example to pray first and then act. This is what Esther did, and Yahweh answered her request. Still, Esther had to do her part too. Reading the rest of the book of Esther confirms that she did not merely pray and then sit back to wait for God to act. She prayed and then took bold action, even at the risk of execution.

Does our understanding of God expect him to do all the work? Are we willing to do what we can and trust God with what we can't?

May we place our trust in God for our future and our fate.

Psalm 178:

Job's Lament

Job 1:21

Granted limited authorization by God, Satan afflicts Job, taking away his possessions and killing all ten of his children. Job humbles himself—tearing his robe and shaving his head. He falls to the ground and worships the Almighty.

From the angst of his pain, he succinctly summarizes the arc of his life, affirms God's sovereignty, and blesses Yahweh.

Though his words are few, it may be all he can muster at this low point in his life. What he says emerges as a psalm of lament.

> "Naked I came out of my mother's womb, and naked will I return there. Yahweh gave, and Yahweh has taken away. Blessed be Yahweh's name."

Reflection: Job didn't realize that it was Satan who afflicted him. He assumed it was Yahweh's doing. He also didn't know that God placed limits on the harm Satan could inflict on him.

As with Job's case, we're seldom privy to what happens in the spiritual realm, seeing only what physically occurs around us. Though we see in part, we can trust God, through faith, that the rest will work out (see Romans 8:28).

Do we trust God with our life—every part of it? When disaster strikes, do we blame Yahweh or bless him?

May we learn from the life of Job and apply those insights to our life today.

Psalm 179:

Job Speaks to God

Job 42:2–6

The book of Job records dialogue between Job and his four friends. Each one offers him their perspective on the situation—through their limited theology. To varying degrees, all four assert that Job's downfall is either his fault or God's doing.

Job disagrees, maintains his innocence, and proclaims God's blamelessness. He has questions for sure, but in making his inquiries of God, he does so with a right perspective that God appreciates.

God gives a lengthy response to Job and his four friends, primarily to the four friends. Yet Job receives God's words as a mortifying rebuke. He humbles himself before his Lord and offers this psalm of contrition.

> "I know that you can do all things,
> and that no purpose of yours can be restrained.
> You asked, 'Who is this who hides counsel
> without knowledge?'

therefore I have uttered that which I didn't understand,
things too wonderful for me, which I didn't know.
You said, 'Listen, now, and I will speak;
I will question you, and you will answer me.'
I had heard of you by the hearing of the ear,
but now my eye sees you.
Therefore I abhor myself,
and repent in dust and ashes."

Reflection: Job endured much at Satan's hand. Nevertheless, Job remained true to his Lord despite much suffering, and God blessed him by restoring what he lost twofold.

Regardless of what befalls us, are we able to endure it without sinning, as Job did? Though God can restore to us what we've lost, will we remain true to him even if he doesn't?

May our confidence in Yahweh never waver.

Psalm 180:

To Everything There Is a Season

Ecclesiastes 3:1–8

The book of Ecclesiastes shares Solomon's personal journey of trying to find meaning and purpose in his life. It's a dismal saga, discouraging and void of hope.

Early on Solomon shares a pessimistic view about the seasons of life. He opens acknowledging there's a time to be born and a time to die. He ends the passage stating there's a time for war and a time for peace. If someone wasn't discouraged before reading Ecclesiastes, Solomon's words could easily bring them to that point.

We'll treat this passage as a psalm, a song even. Others have done just that, with the song becoming an international hit by The Byrds in 1965.

Here is the biblical portion of this psalm turned hit song.

For everything there is a season, and a time for
every purpose under heaven:
a time to be born,
and a time to die;
a time to plant,
and a time to pluck up that which is planted;
a time to kill,
and a time to heal;
a time to break down,
and a time to build up;
a time to weep,
and a time to laugh;
a time to mourn,
and a time to dance;
a time to cast away stones,
and a time to gather stones together;
a time to embrace,
and a time to refrain from embracing;
a time to seek,
and a time to lose;
a time to keep,
and a time to cast away;
a time to tear,
and a time to sew;
a time to keep silence,
and a time to speak;
a time to love,

and a time to hate;
a time for war,
and a time for peace.

Reflection: Similar to the perplexing nature of this passage, weaving its way throughout the book of Ecclesiastes is a meandering path of discouragement and disillusionment. Given this, it's easy to miss the last two verses of the book, which put everything into perspective: Solomon concludes his search for meaning by saying that we are to fear God and obey his commands; this is our duty—the meaning and purpose of life (see Ecclesiastes 12:13–14).

Does this psalm from Ecclesiastes lift us up or pull us down? Does it fill us with hope or overwhelm us with despair? What role does God play in our answers? What role *should* he play?

May our purpose in life be to love God and obey him.

Psalm 181:

Jonah's Testimony

Jonah 2:2–9

After disobeying God and running away from what he was supposed to do, we know that Jonah spends a three-day timeout in the belly of a large fish. From this dire location, he prays. Jonah's prayer is a poetic testimony of what he did and the disaster that followed because of his disobedience and being in the wrong place.

It's worth pointing out that, even though Jonah is still in the belly of the fish, he first affirms that God heard him. The wayward prophet then ends his prayer with the acknowledgment that God will save him.

"I called because of my affliction to Yahweh.
He answered me.
Out of the belly of Sheol I cried.
You heard my voice.
For you threw me into the depths,
in the heart of the seas.
The flood was all around me.
All your waves and your billows passed over me.
I said, 'I have been banished from your sight;

yet I will look again toward your holy temple.'
The waters surrounded me,
even to the soul.
The deep was around me.
The weeds were wrapped around my head.
I went down to the bottoms of the mountains.
The earth barred me in forever:
yet have you brought up my life from the pit,
Yahweh my God.

"When my soul fainted within me, I remembered
Yahweh.
My prayer came in to you, into your holy temple.
Those who regard lying vanities forsake their own
mercy.
But I will sacrifice to you with the voice of
thanksgiving.
I will pay that which I have vowed.
Salvation belongs to Yahweh."

Reflection: Jonah didn't seek God until it looked like he was about to die. Instead of running off in the opposite direction, what if he had prayed for courage when God first spoke to him and told him to go to Nineveh? Instead, Jonah acted first and then prayed.

When have we acted on our own and then resorted to prayer to get us out of a jam? Do we believe Yahweh will *always* rescue us from our folly? Should we?

May we always seek God first.

Psalm 182:

Angels Sing Praise

Isaiah 6:3

The next nine psalms come from the book of Isaiah. Isaiah writes in Judah during the reigns of kings Uzziah, Jotham, Ahaz, and Hezekiah. During Isaiah's lengthy time as a prophet, Assyria conquers the nation of Israel and exiles most of the people. Only the nation of Judah remains, which split from Israel a couple centuries before.

In less than one hundred years, the nation of Babylon will likewise conquer Judah and exile them too. (Which we will see when we explore the psalms in the book of Jeremiah.)

Both nations fall due to their repeated disregard of God and his commands.

This is the context for Isaiah's and Jeremiah's writing and the psalms that their books contain. With this background, let's consider Isaiah's first contribution to our collection.

Not all psalms of praise need to come from people. Angels can praise God too.

Isaiah relates an experience of hearing angels chant their adoration to their Creator. We don't know if this comes to Isaiah in the form of a vision or if his spirit ascends for a time into heaven to witness this. What we do know is how the angels worship God in an interactive form of adulation, repeating this phrase to one another:

> "Holy, holy, holy, is Yahweh of Armies!
> The whole earth is full of his glory!"

Reflection: Imagine the angels chanting this to one another. These words could come at various volumes, with different timing, and harmonizing with all the vocal ranges. The mantra rises and falls, building to a crescendo where the angels turn as one to Yahweh and offer their praise to him as he listens.

At this point, the temple on earth rattles and fills with smoke. Overwhelmed, Isaiah says, "Woe is me. I've seen the Lord God." He feels unworthy, a man of unclean lips.

Though we may never have an experience like Isaiah's, how might we respond to the presence of God's overwhelming glory? Do we see ourselves joining the angels in praise or pulling back as undeserving and with overwhelming fear?

May we elevate our worship of Yahweh to acknowledge and praise his holiness, just like these angels.

Psalm 183:

The People's Song of Praise

Isaiah 12:1–6

As we move through the book of Isaiah, the prophet offers a future glimpse of Jesus reaching out to embrace people of all nations, not just Israel. In response to this, Isaiah envisions a future people joining to sing this psalm of praise to God:

> "I will give thanks to you, Yahweh; for though you were angry with me, your anger has turned away and you comfort me. Behold, God is my salvation. I will trust, and will not be afraid; for Yah, Yahweh, is my strength and song; and he has become my salvation . . . ."

> "Give thanks to Yahweh! Call on his name! Declare his doings among the peoples! Proclaim that his name is exalted! Sing to Yahweh, for he

> has done excellent things! Let this be known in all the earth! Cry aloud and shout, you inhabitant of Zion; for the Holy One of Israel is great among you!"

Reflection: Though God's chosen people thought he was Lord only for their nation, the Old Testament overflows with hints that he intended to save all people.

Do we thank God (Jesus) for our salvation? How can we spread this good news throughout the earth, to *all* peoples?

May we follow Jesus and be his disciple.

Psalm 184:

Confident in God

Isaiah 25:1–12

A psalm can contain prophecy. And a prophecy can read like a psalm, but the two don't usually overlap.

After Isaiah prophesies about the earth's devastation in Isaiah 24 (which we're not treating as a psalm), he affirms that through it all God will continue to reign with great glory. What follows that passage is this confident psalm of praise.

> Yahweh, you are my God. I will exalt you! I will praise your name, for you have done wonderful things, things planned long ago, in complete faithfulness and truth. For you have made a city into a heap, a fortified city into a ruin, a palace of strangers to be no city. It will never be built. Therefore a strong people will glorify you. A city of awesome nations will fear you. For you

have been a stronghold to the poor, a stronghold to the needy in his distress, a refuge from the storm, a shade from the heat, when the blast of the dreaded ones is like a storm against the wall. As the heat in a dry place you will bring down the noise of strangers; as the heat by the shade of a cloud, the song of the dreaded ones will be brought low.

In this mountain, Yahweh of Armies will make all peoples a feast of choice meat, a feast of choice wines, of choice meat full of marrow, of well refined choice wines. He will destroy in this mountain the surface of the covering that covers all peoples, and the veil that is spread over all nations. He has swallowed up death forever! The Lord Yahweh will wipe away tears from off all faces. He will take the reproach of his people away from off all the earth, for Yahweh has spoken it.

It shall be said in that day, "Behold, this is our God! We have waited for him, and he will save us! This is Yahweh! We have waited for him. We will be glad and rejoice in his salvation!" For Yahweh's hand will rest in this mountain.

> Moab will be trodden down in his place, even like straw is trodden down in the water of the dunghill. He will spread out his hands in the middle of it, like one who swims spreads out hands to swim, but his pride will be humbled together with the craft of his hands. He has brought the high fortress of your walls down, laid low, and brought to the ground, even to the dust.

Reflection: Isaiah receives a disheartening prophecy from God. The prophet's reaction is to write this psalm of adoration for the Almighty. Though later verses include some prophecy as well, it overflows with confidence in Yahweh's character.

When we receive discouraging news, how do we respond? Do we blame God? Or do we praise his character, confident that he will provide?

May our response to discouragement honor Yahweh and point others to him.

Psalm 185:

A Song of Praise

Isaiah 26:1–21

Isaiah follows one psalm with another, this one also a song of praise. Just like the passage that precedes it, he thanks God for his redemption.

> "We have a strong city.
> God appoints salvation for walls and bulwarks.
> Open the gates, that the righteous nation may enter:
> the one which keeps faith.
> You will keep whoever's mind is steadfast in perfect peace,
> because he trusts in you.
> Trust in Yahweh forever;
> for in Yah, Yahweh, is an everlasting Rock.
> For he has brought down those who dwell on high, the lofty city.
> He lays it low.

He lays it low even to the ground.
He brings it even to the dust.
The foot shall tread it down,
even the feet of the poor
and the steps of the needy."
The way of the just is uprightness.
You who are upright make the path of the righteous level.

Yes, in the way of your judgments, Yahweh, we have waited for you.
Your name and your renown are the desire of our soul.
With my soul I have desired you in the night.
Yes, with my spirit within me I will seek you earnestly;
for when your judgments are in the earth, the inhabitants of the world learn righteousness.
Let favor be shown to the wicked,
yet he will not learn righteousness.
In the land of uprightness he will deal wrongfully,
and will not see Yahweh's majesty.

Yahweh, your hand is lifted up, yet they don't see;
but they will see your zeal for the people, and be disappointed.
Yes, fire will consume your adversaries.

Yahweh, you will ordain peace for us,
for you have also done all our work for us.
Yahweh our God, other lords besides you have had dominion over us,
but we will only acknowledge your name.
The dead shall not live.
The departed spirits shall not rise.
Therefore you have visited and destroyed them,
and caused all memory of them to perish.
You have increased the nation, O Yahweh.
You have increased the nation!
You are glorified!
You have enlarged all the borders of the land.

Yahweh, in trouble they have visited you.
They poured out a prayer when your chastening was on them.
Just as a woman with child, who draws near the time of her delivery,
is in pain and cries out in her pangs,
so we have been before you, Yahweh.
We have been with child.
We have been in pain.
We gave birth, it seems, only to wind.
We have not worked any deliverance in the earth;
neither have the inhabitants of the world fallen.

Your dead shall live.
My dead bodies shall arise.
Awake and sing, you who dwell in the dust;
for your dew is like the dew of herbs,
and the earth will cast out the departed spirits.

Come, my people, enter into your rooms,
and shut your doors behind you.
Hide yourself for a little moment,
until the indignation is past.
For, behold, Yahweh comes out of his place to punish the inhabitants of the earth for their iniquity.
The earth also will disclose her blood, and will no longer cover her slain.

Reflection: This psalm of praise has an overall arc of redemption, but it also contains other evocative images such as a consuming fire and a woman giving birth.

Do we trust Yahweh for our salvation? Our redemption? What other phrase or idea can we take from this psalm to encourage us in how we live today and hope for tomorrow?

May we trust Yahweh to save us.

Psalm 186:

Hezekiah's Lament and Praise

Isaiah 38:10–20

Three books in the Bible record the life of King Hezekiah. We can read his story in 2 Kings 18–20, 2 Chronicles 29–32, and Isaiah 36–38. Each passage covers similar information, yet each also provides unique content. All three talk about an illness that brings Hezekiah close to death.

The passages in 2 Kings and Isaiah give additional information. In these accounts, Isaiah goes to the king and tells him to put his house in order, for he will soon die. Weeping, Hezekiah seeks Yahweh, asking him for a reprieve.

Right away Isaiah receives an update from God.

God now promises that Hezekiah will recover from his near-fatal illness and live another fifteen years. But Hezekiah asks Isaiah for a sign that this will happen. This request makes sense because in the span of a few minutes, Isaiah had delivered conflicting words to the king.

To confirm that the second prophecy supersedes the first, God causes the sun to travel backward for a time to prove that Hezekiah's recovery will take place. Hezekiah recuperates, as promised, and the king lives fifteen more years.

After Hezekiah's recovery, he pens this psalm of praise to God:

> I said, "In the middle of my life I go into the gates of Sheol.
> I am deprived of the residue of my years."
> I said, "I won't see Yah,
> Yah in the land of the living.
> I will see man no more with the inhabitants of the world.
> My dwelling is removed,
> and is carried away from me like a shepherd's tent.
> I have rolled up my life like a weaver.
> He will cut me off from the loom.
> From day even to night you will make an end of me.
> I waited patiently until morning.
> He breaks all my bones like a lion.

From day even to night you will make an end of me.
I chattered like a swallow or a crane.
I moaned like a dove.
My eyes weaken looking upward.
Lord, I am oppressed.
Be my security."
What will I say?
He has both spoken to me, and himself has done it.
I will walk carefully all my years because of the anguish of my soul.
Lord, men live by these things;
and my spirit finds life in all of them:
you restore me, and cause me to live.
Behold, for peace I had great anguish,
but you have in love for my soul delivered it from the pit of corruption;
for you have cast all my sins behind your back.
For Sheol can't praise you.
Death can't celebrate you.
Those who go down into the pit can't hope for your truth.
The living, the living, he shall praise you, as I do today.
The father shall make known your truth to the children.

Yahweh will save me.
Therefore we will sing my songs with stringed instruments all the days of our life in Yahweh's house.

Reflection: When God tells Hezekiah he will soon die, the king doesn't accept it. Instead, he seeks the Almighty and asks for more time. God changes his mind and blesses Hezekiah with another fifteen years.

Do we believe that God still changes his mind today? Have we ever heard conflicting instructions from him? What do we do to reconcile this? When we receive discouraging news, do we accept it as inevitable or seek God's intervention?

May we discern when to ask Yahweh for a reprieve and when to accept what he decrees.

Psalm 187:

Isaiah's Prophetic Psalm

Isaiah 40:3–31

Several of the Psalms have prophetic elements. This passage is an example of prophecy that reads like a psalm.

Here is Isaiah's prophetic psalm:

The voice of one who calls out,
"Prepare the way of Yahweh in the wilderness!
Make a level highway in the desert for our God.
Every valley shall be exalted,
and every mountain and hill shall be made low.
The uneven shall be made level,
and the rough places a plain.
Yahweh's glory shall be revealed,
and all flesh shall see it together;
for the mouth of Yahweh has spoken it."

The voice of one saying, "Cry!"
One said, "What shall I cry?"
"All flesh is like grass,
and all its glory is like the flower of the field.
The grass withers,
the flower fades,
because Yahweh's breath blows on it.
Surely the people are like grass.
The grass withers,
the flower fades;
but the word of our God stands forever."

You who tell good news to Zion, go up on a high mountain.
You who tell good news to Jerusalem, lift up your voice with strength!
Lift it up! Don't be afraid!
Say to the cities of Judah, "Behold, your God!"
Behold, the Lord Yahweh will come as a mighty one,
and his arm will rule for him.
Behold, his reward is with him,
and his recompense before him.
He will feed his flock like a shepherd.
He will gather the lambs in his arm,
and carry them in his bosom.

He will gently lead those who have their young.

Who has measured the waters in the hollow of his hand,
and marked off the sky with his span,
and calculated the dust of the earth in a measuring basket,
and weighed the mountains in scales,
and the hills in a balance?
Who has directed Yahweh's Spirit,
or has taught him as his counselor?
Who did he take counsel with,
and who instructed him,
and taught him in the path of justice,
and taught him knowledge,
and showed him the way of understanding?
Behold, the nations are like a drop in a bucket,
and are regarded as a speck of dust on a balance.
Behold, he lifts up the islands like a very little thing.
Lebanon is not sufficient to burn,
nor its animals sufficient for a burnt offering.
All the nations are like nothing before him.
They are regarded by him as less than nothing, and vanity.

To whom then will you liken God?

Or what likeness will you compare to him?
A workman has cast an image,
and the goldsmith overlays it with gold,
and casts silver chains for it.
He who is too impoverished for such an offering
chooses a tree that will not rot.
He seeks a skillful workman to set up a carved image for him that will not be moved.

Haven't you known?
Haven't you heard?
Haven't you been told from the beginning?
Haven't you understood from the foundations of the earth?
It is he who sits above the circle of the earth,
and its inhabitants are like grasshoppers;
who stretches out the heavens like a curtain,
and spreads them out like a tent to dwell in,
who brings princes to nothing,
who makes the judges of the earth meaningless.
They are planted scarcely.
They are sown scarcely.
Their stock has scarcely taken root in the ground.
He merely blows on them, and they wither,
and the whirlwind takes them away as stubble.

"To whom then will you liken me?
Who is my equal?" says the Holy One.
Lift up your eyes on high,
and see who has created these,
who brings out their army by number.
He calls them all by name.
by the greatness of his might,
and because he is strong in power,
not one is lacking.

Why do you say, Jacob,
and speak, Israel,
"My way is hidden from Yahweh,
and the justice due me is disregarded by my God?"
Haven't you known?
Haven't you heard?
The everlasting God, Yahweh,
the Creator of the ends of the earth, doesn't faint.
He isn't weary.
His understanding is unsearchable.
He gives power to the weak.
He increases the strength of him who has no might.
Even the youths faint and get weary,
and the young men utterly fall;

but those who wait for Yahweh will renew their
strength.
They will mount up with wings like eagles.
They will run, and not be weary.
They will walk, and not faint.

Reflection: It matters not if we consider this passage as prophecy, psalm, or both. What matters is how God speaks to us through these words.

What verses or phrases in this psalm resonate most with you? How can we let them inform—or reform—our understanding of Yahweh and our relationship to him?

May every bit of God's Word speak to us.

Psalm 188:

Song of Praise to God

Isaiah 42:10–13

Though some Psalms quote God, such as Psalms 12, 68, 91, and 110, his direct words are few and fit into the author's overall poetic arc. Isaiah 42 is the opposite, with Isaiah's few words connecting many verses from God. In this case, we'll consider only Isaiah's own words.

Here is his psalm of praise.

Sing to Yahweh a new song,
  and his praise from the end of the earth,
  you who go down to the sea,
  and all that is therein,
  the islands and their inhabitants.
Let the wilderness and its cities raise their voices,
  with the villages that Kedar inhabits.
  Let the inhabitants of Sela sing.
  Let them shout from the top of the mountains!

Let them give glory to Yahweh,
  and declare his praise in the islands.
Yahweh will go out like a mighty man.
  He will stir up zeal like a man of war.
  He will raise a war cry.
  Yes, he will shout aloud.
  He will triumph over his enemies.

Reflection: This psalm opens with instruction to sing a new song to Yahweh. This idea is not unique to Isaiah. Six other Psalms, as well as two references in Revelation (one of which we'll cover in "Psalm 212: A New Song"), talk about giving God a new song.

The Bible never tells us to sing our old favorites but to worship him with something new. How willing are we to praise Yahweh with a *new* song?

Many people love to sing old hymns and familiar choruses. Should we push these aside to sing a new song to God? Maybe. Or perhaps we can honor God simply by singing the old songs in a new way, singing them afresh for him.

May we give the Almighty our best in song and in all we do.

Psalm 189:

Awake and Depart

Isaiah 52:1–15

This is another passage of mixed genres. It reads very much as a psalm, but it also contains prophecy, as well as direct quotes from God.

Awake, awake! Put on your strength, Zion.
  Put on your beautiful garments, Jerusalem, the holy city:
  for from now on the uncircumcised and the unclean will no more come into you.
Shake yourself from the dust!
  Arise, sit up, Jerusalem!
  Release yourself from the bonds of your neck, captive daughter of Zion!

For Yahweh says, "You were sold for nothing;
  and you will be redeemed without money."

For the Lord Yahweh says:

"My people went down at the first into Egypt to live there:
and the Assyrian has oppressed them without cause.

"Now therefore, what do I do here," says Yahweh, "seeing that my people are taken away for nothing?
Those who rule over them mock," says Yahweh, "and my name is blasphemed continually all day long.
Therefore my people shall know my name.
Therefore they shall know in that day that I am he who speaks.
Behold, it is I."

How beautiful on the mountains are the feet of him who brings good news,
who publishes peace,
who brings good news,
who proclaims salvation,
who says to Zion, "Your God reigns!"
Your watchmen lift up their voice.
Together they sing;

for they shall see eye to eye when Yahweh returns to Zion.
Break out into joy!
Sing together, you waste places of Jerusalem;
for Yahweh has comforted his people.
He has redeemed Jerusalem.
Yahweh has made his holy arm bare in the eyes of all the nations.
All the ends of the earth have seen the salvation of our God.

Depart! Depart! Go out from there! Touch no unclean thing!
Go out from among her!
Cleanse yourselves, you who carry Yahweh's vessels.
For you shall not go out in haste,
neither shall you go by flight:
for Yahweh will go before you;
and the God of Israel will be your rear guard.

Behold, my servant will deal wisely.
He will be exalted and lifted up,
and will be very high.
Just as many were astonished at you—
his appearance was marred more than any man,
and his form more than the sons of men—

so he will cleanse many nations.
Kings will shut their mouths at him;
for they will see that which had not been told them,
and they will understand that which they had not heard.

Reflection: We have many things that we can glean from this passage, but notable are two times when Isaiah repeats a word for emphasis. The first is in the opening line that tells us to *awake*. The second—in verse 11—tells us to *depart*. Both are imperative.

Do we need to awake? What might God be calling us to open our eyes to see?

Do we need to depart? Where might God be calling us to go?

May we awake to what Yahweh says and depart to where he says to go.

Psalm 190:

Isaiah's Lament

Isaiah 63:7–19

This psalm takes us on a roller coaster of emotions.

It opens with an inspiring promise to tell others about Yahweh, praising him in the process. The second portion delves into the people's past rebellion and God's subsequent rescue. This seems like an ideal place to end this psalm, but Isaiah continues. He begs for God to consider his people's present plight and deliver them from their sorry existence.

Here is Isaiah's final psalm.

I will tell of the loving kindnesses of Yahweh
and the praises of Yahweh,
according to all that Yahweh has given to us,
and the great goodness toward the house of Israel,

which he has given to them according to his mercies,
and according to the multitude of his loving kindnesses.
For he said, "Surely, they are my people,
children who will not deal falsely;"
so he became their Savior.
In all their affliction he was afflicted,
and the angel of his presence saved them.
In his love and in his pity he redeemed them.
He bore them,
and carried them all the days of old.

But they rebelled
and grieved his Holy Spirit.
Therefore he turned and became their enemy,
and he himself fought against them.

Then he remembered the days of old,
Moses and his people, saying,
"Where is he who brought them up out of the sea
with the shepherds of his flock?
Where is he who put his Holy Spirit among them?"
Who caused his glorious arm to be at Moses' right hand?

Who divided the waters before them, to make
himself an everlasting name?
Who led them through the depths,
like a horse in the wilderness,
so that they didn't stumble?
As the livestock that go down into the valley,
Yahweh's Spirit caused them to rest.
So you led your people to make yourself a
glorious name.

Look down from heaven,
and see from the habitation of your holiness
and of your glory.
Where are your zeal and your mighty acts?
The yearning of your heart and your compassion
is restrained toward me.
For you are our Father,
though Abraham doesn't know us,
and Israel does not acknowledge us.
You, Yahweh, are our Father.
Our Redeemer from everlasting is your name.
O Yahweh, why do you make us wander from
your ways,
and harden our heart from your fear?
Return for your servants' sake,
the tribes of your inheritance.
Your holy people possessed it but a little while.

Our adversaries have trodden down your sanctuary.
We have become like those over whom you never ruled,
like those who were not called by your name.

Reflection: Isaiah's psalm gives us much to contemplate.

Which part of this psalm do you most resonate with? What can we learn from the rest?

May God receive our words as an act of worship and adoration.

Psalm 191:

Request for Deliverance

Jeremiah 10:23–25

Our next two Psalms come from the prophet Jeremiah. His ministry occurs toward the end of the nation of Judah's existence. His book ends with Judah's exile.

In this short psalm, Jeremiah opens with an unassuming gentleness, yet he quickly implores Yahweh to punish those nations and families who oppose him and have afflicted his people.

> Yahweh, I know that the way of man is not in himself.
> It is not in man who walks to direct his steps.
> Yahweh, correct me, but gently;
> not in your anger,
> lest you reduce me to nothing.
> Pour out your wrath on the nations that don't know you,

and on the families that don't call on your name;
for they have devoured Jacob.
Yes, they have devoured him, consumed him,
and have laid waste his habitation.

Reflection: Jeremiah asks Yahweh to treat him gently and punish his enemies harshly.

Do we expect to receive God's mercy while at the same time calling for him to judge others?

May we want God's grace for others as much as for ourselves. After all, everyone sins and needs Jesus. This includes us, and it includes our enemies too.

Psalm 192:

Jeremiah's Complaint

Jeremiah 20:7–18

Jeremiah, God's prophet, proclaims his Lord's words. When Pashhur, the priest in charge of the temple, hears Jeremiah predicting destruction, he has the prophet beaten and thrown in stocks for a day. Upon his release, Jeremiah foretells that because Pashhur prophesied lies, he, his family, and all who listen to him will be exiled to Babylon, where they will die.

After this bold declaration, Jeremiah pens this psalm of despair.

Yahweh, you have persuaded me, and I was persuaded.
You are stronger than I, and have prevailed.
I have become a laughingstock all day.
Everyone mocks me.
For as often as I speak, I cry out;
I cry, "Violence and destruction!"

because Yahweh's word has been made a reproach
  to me,
 and a derision, all day.
If I say, I will not make mention of him,
 or speak any more in his name,
then there is in my heart as it were a burning fire
  shut up in my bones.
 I am weary with holding it in.
 I can't.
For I have heard the defaming of many,
 "Terror on every side!
 Denounce, and we will denounce him!"
say all my familiar friends,
 those who watch for my fall.
"Perhaps he will be persuaded,
 and we will prevail against him,
 and we will take our revenge on him."
But Yahweh is with me as an awesome mighty
  one.
 Therefore my persecutors will stumble,
 and they won't prevail.
They will be utterly disappointed,
 because they have not dealt wisely,
 even with an everlasting dishonor which will
  never be forgotten.
But Yahweh of Armies, who tests the righteous,
 who sees the heart and the mind,

let me see your vengeance on them,
  for I have revealed my cause to you.
Sing to Yahweh!
  Praise Yahweh,
  for he has delivered the soul of the needy from the hand of evildoers.
Cursed is the day in which I was born.
  Don't let the day in which my mother bore me be blessed.
Cursed is the man who brought news to my father, saying,
  "A boy is born to you," making him very glad.
Let that man be as the cities which Yahweh overthrew,
  and didn't repent.
Let him hear a cry in the morning,
  and shouting at noontime;
because he didn't kill me from the womb.
  So my mother would have been my grave,
  and her womb always great.
Why did I come out of the womb to see labor and sorrow,
  that my days should be consumed with shame?

Reflection: Jeremiah proclaimed God's word, as instructed, and a religious leader persecuted him for it.

When have we suffered for doing what was right? For obeying God and what he told us to do?

May we always relish the life Yahweh gave us.

[If you, like Jeremiah, wish that you were never born, know that God has a better plan for you. Seek help from a trusted friend or God-honoring counselor. With their help—and God's—you can move to embrace a better tomorrow.]

Psalm 193:

A Lament of Desolation

Lamentations 1

The book of Lamentations serves mainly as a postscript to the book of Jeremiah. It consists of five funeral dirges that mourn the loss of Jerusalem, as proclaimed in Jeremiah's prophecy. Many Bible scholars consider Jeremiah to be the author of Lamentations, and some ancient translations list the book's title as the "Lamentations of Jeremiah."

We can read these five psalms of lament as a progression, a story arc that begins with Jerusalem's fall and ends with a response from those who remain. Throughout this, God is central. We must take care, however, to not build our understanding of God based on how the author perceives him in these poems. Instead, we should receive these words as a reflection of the writer's deepest despair.

The first four of the five chapters (laments) are acrostic poems in Hebrew, with each verse beginning with a successive letter in the 22-character Hebrew alphabet. Though this structure has no real impact when we read these psalms in English, it confirms the forethought and intentionality of the author.

The first psalm in Lamentations, corresponding to the first chapter of the book, focuses on the fall of Jerusalem and the resulting desolation. It stands as an apt poetic funeral dirge to the central city of the nation of God's chosen people.

It's a solemn reminder of what happens when we ignore Yahweh.

> How the city sits solitary,
>   that was full of people!
> She has become as a widow,
>   who was great among the nations!
> She who was a princess among the provinces
>   has become a slave!
>
> She weeps bitterly in the night.
>   Her tears are on her cheeks.
> Among all her lovers
>   she has no one to comfort her.
> All her friends have dealt treacherously with her.
>   They have become her enemies.

Judah has gone into captivity because of affliction,
and because of great servitude.
She dwells among the nations.
She finds no rest.
All her persecutors overtook her within the straits.

The roads to Zion mourn,
because no one comes to the solemn assembly.
All her gates are desolate.
Her priests sigh.
Her virgins are afflicted,
and she herself is in bitterness.

Her adversaries have become the head.
Her enemies prosper;
for Yahweh has afflicted her for the multitude of her transgressions.
Her young children have gone into captivity before the adversary.

All majesty has departed from the daughter of Zion.
Her princes have become like deer that find no pasture.
They have gone without strength before the pursuer.

Jerusalem remembers in the days of her affliction
and of her miseries
all her pleasant things that were from the days
of old;
when her people fell into the hand of the
adversary,
and no one helped her.
The adversaries saw her.
They mocked at her desolations.

Jerusalem has grievously sinned.
Therefore she has become unclean.
All who honored her despise her,
because they have seen her nakedness.
Yes, she sighs, and turns backward.

Her filthiness was in her skirts.
She didn't remember her latter end.
Therefore she has come down astoundingly.
She has no comforter.
"See, Yahweh, my affliction;
for the enemy has magnified himself."

The adversary has spread out his hand on all her
pleasant things;
for she has seen that the nations have entered
into her sanctuary,

concerning whom you commanded that they
should not enter into your assembly.

All her people sigh.
They seek bread.
They have given their pleasant things for food
to refresh their soul.
"Look, Yahweh, and see;
for I have become despised."

"Is it nothing to you, all you who pass by?
Look, and see if there is any sorrow like my
sorrow,
which is brought on me,
with which Yahweh has afflicted me in the day
of his fierce anger.

"From on high has he sent fire into my bones,
and it prevails against them.
He has spread a net for my feet.
He has turned me back.
He has made me desolate and I faint all day
long.

"The yoke of my transgressions is bound by his
hand.
They are knit together.

They have come up on my neck.
He made my strength fail.
The Lord has delivered me into their hands,
against whom I am not able to stand.

"The Lord has set at nothing all my mighty men within me.
He has called a solemn assembly against me to crush my young men.
The Lord has trodden the virgin daughter of Judah as in a wine press.

"For these things I weep.
My eye, my eye runs down with water,
because the comforter who should refresh my soul is far from me.
My children are desolate,
because the enemy has prevailed."

Zion spreads out her hands.
There is no one to comfort her.
Yahweh has commanded concerning Jacob,
that those who are around him should be his adversaries.
Jerusalem is among them as an unclean thing.

"Yahweh is righteous;
for I have rebelled against his commandment.

Please hear all you peoples,
and see my sorrow.
My virgins and my young men have gone into captivity.

"I called for my lovers,
but they deceived me.
My priests and my elders gave up the spirit in the city,
while they sought food for themselves to refresh their souls.

"Look, Yahweh; for I am in distress.
My heart is troubled.
My heart turns over within me,
for I have grievously rebelled.
Abroad, the sword bereaves.
At home, it is like death.

"They have heard that I sigh.
There is no one to comfort me.
All my enemies have heard of my trouble.
They are glad that you have done it.
You will bring the day that you have proclaimed,
and they will be like me.

"Let all their wickedness come before you.

Do to them as you have done to me for all my
transgressions.
For my sighs are many,
and my heart is faint.

Reflection: Yahweh repeatedly warned his children what would happen if they disregarded his words. Throughout the centuries, they received some punishment for their disobedience, but God offered them much more mercy than judgment.

However, at last, judgment remains the only option. Jerusalem falls. The kingdom of God's people ends.

Hidden in the middle of this agonizing poem is the line "She didn't remember her latter end." That is, the people of Jerusalem didn't consider their future. In effect, they lived for today without a care for the consequences of their actions. Yet consequences caught up with them.

Do we have a future-focused perspective or a live-for-today mentality? Do we expect to receive God's mercy and dismiss his judgment?

May a God-honoring perspective cover our life today and our outlook for tomorrow.

Psalm 194:

A Lament of Judgment

Lamentations 2

As we move from the first psalm of lament to the second, the focus shifts to God's judgment of the city and his people who live there. From this passage it would be easy to conclude that Yahweh is a mean, vindictive, judgmental deity.

Yet if we pull back and look at the big picture, we see a God who lovingly offered mercy to his people when they deserved punishment. Over the centuries, his patience abounded. Only now, after repeated threats from multiple prophets, does God follow through on the judgment he continually warned his people about, which started in the time of Moses and continued over the centuries through to Jeremiah.

Collectively, the people didn't listen—and now they lament what happened:

How has the Lord covered the daughter of Zion
with a cloud in his anger!

He has cast the beauty of Israel down from heaven to the earth,
and hasn't remembered his footstool in the day of his anger.

The Lord has swallowed up all the dwellings of Jacob
without pity.
He has thrown down in his wrath the strongholds of the daughter of Judah.
He has brought them down to the ground.
He has profaned the kingdom and its princes.

He has cut off all the horn of Israel in fierce anger.
He has drawn back his right hand from before the enemy.
He has burned up Jacob like a flaming fire,
which devours all around.

He has bent his bow like an enemy.
He has stood with his right hand as an adversary.
He has killed all that were pleasant to the eye.
In the tent of the daughter of Zion, he has poured out his wrath like fire.

The Lord has become as an enemy.
He has swallowed up Israel.
He has swallowed up all her palaces.
He has destroyed his strongholds.
He has multiplied mourning and lamentation in the daughter of Judah.

He has violently taken away his tabernacle, as if it were a garden.
He has destroyed his place of assembly.
Yahweh has caused solemn assembly and Sabbath to be forgotten in Zion.
In the indignation of his anger, he has despised the king and the priest.

The Lord has cast off his altar.
He has abhorred his sanctuary.
He has given the walls of her palaces into the hand of the enemy.
They have made a noise in Yahweh's house,
as in the day of a solemn assembly.

Yahweh has purposed to destroy the wall of the daughter of Zion.
He has stretched out the line.
He has not withdrawn his hand from destroying;

He has made the rampart and wall lament.
They languish together.

Her gates have sunk into the ground.
He has destroyed and broken her bars.
Her king and her princes are among the nations where the law is not.
Yes, her prophets find no vision from Yahweh.

The elders of the daughter of Zion sit on the ground.
They keep silence.
They have cast up dust on their heads.
They have clothed themselves with sackcloth.
The virgins of Jerusalem hang down their heads to the ground.

My eyes fail with tears.
My heart is troubled.
My liver is poured on the earth,
because of the destruction of the daughter of my people,
because the young children and the infants swoon in the streets of the city.

They ask their mothers,
"Where is grain and wine?"

when they swoon as the wounded in the streets
of the city,
when their soul is poured out into their
mothers' bosom.

What shall I testify to you?
What shall I liken to you, daughter of Jerusalem?
What shall I compare to you,
that I may comfort you, virgin daughter of
Zion?
For your breach is as big as the sea.
Who can heal you?

Your prophets have seen false and foolish visions
for you.
They have not uncovered your iniquity,
to reverse your captivity,
but have seen for you false revelations and
causes of banishment.

All that pass by clap their hands at you.
They hiss and wag their head at the daughter
of Jerusalem, saying,
"Is this the city that men called 'The perfection
of beauty,
the joy of the whole earth'?"

All your enemies have opened their mouth wide
against you.
They hiss and gnash their teeth.
They say, "We have swallowed her up.
Certainly this is the day that we looked for.
We have found it.
We have seen it."

Yahweh has done that which he planned.
He has fulfilled his word that he commanded
in the days of old.
He has thrown down,
and has not pitied.
He has caused the enemy to rejoice over you.
He has exalted the horn of your adversaries.

Their heart cried to the Lord.
O wall of the daughter of Zion,
let tears run down like a river day and night.
Give yourself no relief.
Don't let your eyes rest.

Arise, cry out in the night,
at the beginning of the watches!
Pour out your heart like water before the face of
the Lord.

Lift up your hands toward him for the life of your young children,
who faint for hunger at the head of every street.

"Look, Yahweh, and see to whom you have done thus!
Should the women eat their offspring,
the children that they held and bounced on their knees?
Should the priest and the prophet be killed in the sanctuary of the Lord?

"The youth and the old man lie on the ground in the streets.
My virgins and my young men have fallen by the sword.
You have killed them in the day of your anger.
You have slaughtered, and not pitied.

"You have called, as in the day of a solemn assembly, my terrors on every side.
There was no one that escaped or remained in the day of Yahweh's anger.
My enemy has consumed those whom I have cared for and brought up.

Reflection: From our perspective today it's easy to understand why God finally punished his people. I doubt anyone would have been as patient with them as Yahweh was. Yet this caught his people off guard—even though they shouldn't have been. Their understandable response is to mourn the disaster that befell them, blaming Yahweh for turning his back on them.

When awful things happen to us, do we blame God for our misfortune? What can we do to better understand God's big-picture perspective when all we want to do is complain about our situation?

May we maintain an unwavering confidence in who Yahweh is and the plan he has for our lives—even if it feels like punishment.

Psalm 195:

A Lament from Jeremiah

Lamentations 3

For the third of our five psalms of lament, we read the author's bitter angst. The prophet Jeremiah did everything that God told him to do, even though he encountered opposition and imprisonment for his obedience.

Though we might expect the prophet to stand at a distance and effectively say to the people, "See, I told you so. I warned you, but you wouldn't listen," Jeremiah doesn't. He carries God's fulfillment of his words as a weight, a personal burden that he cannot bear.

This poem captures the long-suffering prophet's agony.

> I am the man who has seen affliction
>   by the rod of his wrath.
> He has led me and caused me to walk in darkness,
>   and not in light.

Surely he turns his hand against me
again and again all day long.

He has made my flesh and my skin old.
He has broken my bones.
He has built against me,
and surrounded me with bitterness and hardship.
He has made me dwell in dark places,
as those who have been long dead.

He has walled me about, so that I can't go out.
He has made my chain heavy.
Yes, when I cry, and call for help,
he shuts out my prayer.
He has walled up my ways with cut stone.
He has made my paths crooked.

He is to me as a bear lying in wait,
as a lion in secret places.
He has turned away my ways,
and pulled me in pieces.
He has made me desolate.
He has bent his bow,
and set me as a mark for the arrow.

He has caused the shafts of his quiver to enter into my kidneys.
I have become a derision to all my people,
and their song all day long.
He has filled me with bitterness.
He has stuffed me with wormwood.

He has also broken my teeth with gravel.
He has covered me with ashes.
You have removed my soul far away from peace.
I forgot prosperity.
I said, "My strength has perished,
along with my expectation from Yahweh."

Remember my affliction and my misery,
the wormwood and the bitterness.
My soul still remembers them,
and is bowed down within me.
This I recall to my mind;
therefore I have hope.

It is because of Yahweh's loving kindnesses that we are not consumed,
because his compassion doesn't fail.
They are new every morning.
Great is your faithfulness.
"Yahweh is my portion," says my soul.

"Therefore I will hope in him."

Yahweh is good to those who wait for him,
to the soul who seeks him.
It is good that a man should hope
and quietly wait for the salvation of Yahweh.
It is good for a man that he bear the yoke in his youth.

Let him sit alone and keep silence,
because he has laid it on him.
Let him put his mouth in the dust,
if it is so that there may be hope.
Let him give his cheek to him who strikes him.
Let him be filled full of reproach.

For the Lord will not cast off forever.
For though he causes grief,
yet he will have compassion according to the multitude of his loving kindnesses.
For he does not afflict willingly,
nor grieve the children of men.

To crush under foot all the prisoners of the earth,
to turn away the right of a man before the face of the Most High,

to subvert a man in his cause, the Lord doesn't
approve.

Who is he who says, and it comes to pass,
when the Lord doesn't command it?
Doesn't evil and good come out of the mouth of
the Most High?
Why does a living man complain,
a man for the punishment of his sins?

Let us search and try our ways,
and turn again to Yahweh.
Let's lift up our heart with our hands to God in
the heavens.
"We have transgressed and have rebelled.
You have not pardoned.

"You have covered us with anger and pursued us.
You have killed.
You have not pitied.
You have covered yourself with a cloud,
so that no prayer can pass through.
You have made us an off-scouring and refuse
in the middle of the peoples.

"All our enemies have opened their mouth wide
against us.

Terror and the pit have come on us,
devastation and destruction."

My eye runs down with streams of water,
for the destruction of the daughter of my people.
My eye pours down
and doesn't cease,
without any intermission,
until Yahweh looks down,
and sees from heaven.
My eye affects my soul,
because of all the daughters of my city.

They have chased me relentlessly like a bird,
those who are my enemies without cause.
They have cut off my life in the dungeon,
and have cast a stone on me.
Waters flowed over my head.
I said, "I am cut off."

I called on your name, Yahweh,
out of the lowest dungeon.
You heard my voice:
"Don't hide your ear from my sighing,
and my cry."

You came near in the day that I called on you.
  You said, "Don't be afraid."

Lord, you have pleaded the causes of my soul.
  You have redeemed my life.
Yahweh, you have seen my wrong.
  Judge my cause.
You have seen all their vengeance
  and all their plans against me.

You have heard their reproach, Yahweh,
  and all their plans against me,
the lips of those that rose up against me,
  and their plots against me all day long.
You see their sitting down and their rising up.
  I am their song.

You will pay them back, Yahweh,
  according to the work of their hands.
You will give them hardness of heart,
  your curse to them.
You will pursue them in anger,
  and destroy them from under the heavens of Yahweh.

Reflection: Early in this poem, Jeremiah complains that when he calls out for God's help, the Almighty ignores him. Yet midway through, Jeremiah affirms Yahweh's immense love and unfailing compassion. From the depths of his deep despair and his complaint that God is ignoring him, Jeremiah still affirms Yahweh's character.

How do we react when it appears God isn't listening to our prayers? Are we able to affirm his love and compassion regardless of what's happening in our lives?

May we never forget that God loves us and wants the best for us.

Psalm 196:

A Lament of God's Anger

Lamentations 4

As we move forward in the progression of these five psalms of lament, the fourth poem centers on God's anger—or the perception of his anger. It's a heart-wrenching recitation of the outcome of God's wrath.

How the gold has become dim!
The most pure gold has changed!
The stones of the sanctuary are poured out
at the head of every street.

The precious sons of Zion,
comparable to fine gold,
how they are esteemed as earthen pitchers,
the work of the hands of the potter!

Even the jackals offer their breast.
They nurse their young ones.

But the daughter of my people has become cruel,
like the ostriches in the wilderness.

The tongue of the nursing child clings to the roof of his mouth for thirst.
The young children ask bread,
and no one breaks it for them.

Those who ate delicacies are desolate in the streets.
Those who were brought up in purple embrace dunghills.

For the iniquity of the daughter of my people is greater than the sin of Sodom,
which was overthrown as in a moment.
No hands were laid on her.

Her nobles were purer than snow.
They were whiter than milk.
They were more ruddy in body than rubies.
Their polishing was like sapphire.

Their appearance is blacker than a coal.
They are not known in the streets.
Their skin clings to their bones.
It is withered.
It has become like a stick.

Those who are killed with the sword are better
than those who are killed with hunger;
For these pine away, stricken through,
for lack of the fruits of the field.

The hands of the pitiful women have boiled their
own children.
They were their food in the destruction of the
daughter of my people.

Yahweh has accomplished his wrath.
He has poured out his fierce anger.
He has kindled a fire in Zion,
which has devoured its foundations.

The kings of the earth didn't believe,
neither did all the inhabitants of the world,
that the adversary and the enemy would enter
into the gates of Jerusalem.

It is because of the sins of her prophets
and the iniquities of her priests,
that have shed the blood of the just in the
middle of her.

They wander as blind men in the streets.
They are polluted with blood,
So that men can't touch their garments.

"Go away!" they cried to them.
  "Unclean! Go away! Go away! Don't touch!
When they fled away and wandered, men said among the nations,
  "They can't live here any more."

Yahweh's anger has scattered them.
  He will not pay attention to them any more.
They didn't respect the persons of the priests.
  They didn't favor the elders.

Our eyes still fail,
  looking in vain for our help.
  In our watching we have watched for a nation that could not save.

They hunt our steps,
  so that we can't go in our streets.
Our end is near.
  Our days are fulfilled,
  for our end has come.

Our pursuers were swifter than the eagles of the sky.
  They chased us on the mountains.
  They set an ambush for us in the wilderness.

The breath of our nostrils,
  the anointed of Yahweh,
  was taken in their pits;
of whom we said,
    under his shadow we will live among the nations.

Rejoice and be glad, daughter of Edom,
  who dwells in the land of Uz.
The cup will pass through to you also.
  You will be drunken,
  and will make yourself naked.

The punishment of your iniquity is accomplished,
    daughter of Zion.
  He will no more carry you away into captivity.
He will visit your iniquity, daughter of Edom.
  He will uncover your sins.

Reflection: Again, we must remind ourselves that this lament isn't a reflection of Yahweh's character. Instead, it's Jeremiah's perception of what he witnessed.

In the middle of this poem, Jeremiah points the blame at sinful prophets and priests. Yes, greater judgment faces those who lead (see James 3:1). Yet the people who follow these leaders are also culpable for their own sins. That's why everyone received Yahweh's punishment. And that's why everyone *will* receive his punishment—unless they accept Jesus's gift of salvation (Ephesians 2:4–9).

Despite this punishment, however, the psalm concludes with a ray of hope. It affirms that God's punishment has ended.

Do we ever blame our spiritual leaders for our own shortcomings? When we're going through difficulties, do we trust in Yahweh's goodness that our trials will one day end?

May we always keep our focus on God, regardless of what we're going through.

Psalm 197:

A Lament from the Remnant

Lamentations 5

After four acrostic poems, with each verse starting with successive letters from the Hebrew alphabet, our fifth and final psalm of lament is shorter. It reflects the response of the remnant of people who remain in desolated Jerusalem. The rest are either dead or exiled.

Though we may expect this final poem to offer hope, it doesn't. These words merely confirm the people's plaintive condition before a short conclusion ends this final lament.

Remember, Yahweh, what has come on us.
  Look, and see our reproach.
Our inheritance has been turned over to strangers,
  our houses to aliens.
We are orphans and fatherless.

Our mothers are as widows.
We have drunken our water for money.
Our wood is sold to us.
Our pursuers are on our necks.
We are weary, and have no rest.
We have given our hands to the Egyptians,
and to the Assyrians, to be satisfied with bread.
Our fathers sinned, and are no more.
We have borne their iniquities.
Servants rule over us.
There is no one to deliver us out of their hand.
We get our bread at the peril of our lives,
because of the sword of the wilderness.
Our skin is black like an oven,
because of the burning heat of famine.
They ravished the women in Zion,
the virgins in the cities of Judah.
Princes were hanged up by their hands.
The faces of elders were not honored.
The young men carry millstones.
The children stumbled under loads of wood.
The elders have ceased from the gate,
and the young men from their music.
The joy of our heart has ceased.
Our dance is turned into mourning.
The crown has fallen from our head.

Woe to us, for we have sinned!
For this our heart is faint.
For these things our eyes are dim:
for the mountain of Zion, which is desolate.
The foxes walk on it.

You, Yahweh, remain forever.
Your throne is from generation to generation.
Why do you forget us forever,
and forsake us for so long a time?
Turn us to yourself, Yahweh, and we will be turned.
Renew our days as of old.
But you have utterly rejected us.
You are very angry against us.

Reflection: As this poem winds down, the author for a moment affirms Yahweh's eternal existence and everlasting rule. Yet instead of praising him for who he is, the lament leaves us with words such as forget, forsake, reject, and angry. This stands as the people's perception of God. Though it's incorrect, we can understand it given their circumstance.

They briefly plead with Yahweh to return to them and reinstate life as it once was. Yet all they perceive is God's rejection.

When our life is at its worst, what is our view of Yahweh? When we ask the Almighty for a better tomorrow, do we believe he will answer?

May we always place our hope in Yahweh, regardless of the circumstances.

Psalm 198:

Habakkuk's Plea

Habakkuk 1:2–4

Habakkuk's book records a dialogue between him and God, with God's response emerging as prophecy. The book opens with the prophet's plea to God for relief from injustice.

His words flow forth as a psalm of lament:

> Yahweh, how long will I cry, and you will not hear? I cry out to you "Violence!" and will you not save? Why do you show me iniquity, and look at perversity? For destruction and violence are before me. There is strife, and contention rises up. Therefore the law is paralyzed, and justice never prevails; for the wicked surround the righteous; therefore justice comes out perverted.

Reflection: A recurring theme in the Old Testament is justice, with the oppressed calling out to Yahweh for deliverance from the hands of the unjust. Oppression has continued throughout history until now, and we can expect mistreatment to persist until the end of time.

Do we see the injustice in our world today? Do we cry out to Yahweh for relief?

May we lament over the unfair treatment of others and then act to correct it.

Psalm 199:

Habakkuk's Complaint

Habakkuk 1:12–2:1

After Habakkuk cries out to God, God responds. He says to look, watch, and be amazed. But Habakkuk isn't amazed. Perhaps he isn't listening. Or is he too weary to hear?

Habakkuk doesn't respond with a hearty "thank you." Instead, he continues his plea, which we can read as a psalm that reveals the angst of his soul.

> Aren't you from everlasting, Yahweh my God, my Holy One? We will not die. Yahweh, you have appointed him for judgment. You, Rock, have established him to punish. You who have purer eyes than to see evil, and who cannot look on perversity, why do you tolerate those who deal treacherously, and keep silent when the wicked swallows up the man who is more righteous than he, and make men like the fish

> of the sea, like the creeping things, that have no ruler over them? He takes up all of them with the hook. He catches them in his net, and gathers them in his dragnet. Therefore he rejoices and is glad. Therefore he sacrifices to his net, and burns incense to his dragnet, because by them his life is luxurious, and his food is good. Will he therefore continually empty his net, and kill the nations without mercy?

> I will stand at my watch, and set myself on the ramparts, and will look out to see what he will say to me, and what I will answer concerning my complaint.

Reflection: God sometimes seems silent, but we might simply not be hearing him.

Do we ever accuse God of not responding when it might be that we're not listening? In the depth of our despair, are we still willing to praise him?

May we hear Yahweh when he speaks and be ready to do what he says.

Psalm 200:

Habakkuk's Prayer

Habakkuk 3:2–19

The book of Habakkuk concludes with a lengthy prayer that reads like a psalm.

Yahweh, I have heard of your fame.
  I stand in awe of your deeds, Yahweh.
Renew your work in the middle of the years.
  In the middle of the years make it known.
  In wrath, you remember mercy.
God came from Teman,
  the Holy One from Mount Paran. Selah.

His glory covered the heavens,
  and his praise filled the earth.
His splendor is like the sunrise.
  Rays shine from his hand, where his power is hidden.
Plague went before him,

and pestilence followed his feet.
He stood, and shook the earth.
He looked, and made the nations tremble.
The ancient mountains were crumbled.
The age-old hills collapsed.
His ways are eternal.
I saw the tents of Cushan in affliction.
The dwellings of the land of Midian trembled.
Was Yahweh displeased with the rivers?
Was your anger against the rivers,
or your wrath against the sea,
that you rode on your horses,
on your chariots of salvation?
You uncovered your bow.
You called for your sworn arrows. Selah.
You split the earth with rivers.
The mountains saw you, and were afraid.
The storm of waters passed by.
The deep roared and lifted up its hands on high.
The sun and moon stood still in the sky,
at the light of your arrows as they went,
at the shining of your glittering spear.
You marched through the land in wrath.
You threshed the nations in anger.
You went out for the salvation of your people,
for the salvation of your anointed.

You crushed the head of the land of wickedness.
You stripped them head to foot. Selah.

You pierced the heads of his warriors with their own spears.
They came as a whirlwind to scatter me,
gloating as if to devour the wretched in secret.
You trampled the sea with your horses,
churning mighty waters.
I heard, and my body trembled.
My lips quivered at the voice.
Rottenness enters into my bones, and I tremble in my place,
because I must wait quietly for the day of trouble,
for the coming up of the people who invade us.
For though the fig tree doesn't flourish,
nor fruit be in the vines;
the labor of the olive fails,
the fields yield no food;
the flocks are cut off from the fold,
and there is no herd in the stalls:
yet I will rejoice in Yahweh.
I will be joyful in the God of my salvation!
Yahweh, the Lord, is my strength.
He makes my feet like deer's feet,
and enables me to go in high places.

Reflection: This psalm opens with praise to Yahweh and concludes with a confident affirmation, but not before we see the author's deep disappointment, implicitly with God. The key word that connects Habakkuk's discontent with his powerful conclusion is "yet."

Though Habakkuk is frustrated with his reality and, perhaps, by God's response to his pleas, the prophet commits to rejoicing and being filled with joy for God who provides his salvation.

When faced with discouragement, are we able to join Habakkuk in saying, "yet will I rejoice"? Or do we rail against God for not meeting our expectations?

May we rejoice in Yahweh regardless of the season or our situation.

Psalm 201:

Daniel Blesses God

Daniel 2:20–23

Deported from Judah by King Nebuchadnezzar, the prophet Daniel now lives in exile in Babylon in service to its rulers. Our next three psalms come from the book of Daniel, though he only wrote one of them.

Here is the background of the first psalm.

King Nebuchadnezzar has a disturbing dream. He seeks an interpretation from his company of wise men but refuses to tell them what he dreamt. He demands they prove their abilities to interpret his dream by first telling him what the dream was.

No one can.

Nebuchadnezzar is furious and orders their execution. This decree includes Daniel and his three friends, even though they knew nothing of the situation.

When Daniel hears the details, he asks for time so that he may interpret the dream. He and his three friends plead with God for the revelation. Supernatural insight comes to Daniel that night in a vision and as a result, he praises God in this psalm.

> "Blessed be the name of God forever and ever;
>   for wisdom and might are his.
> He changes the times and the seasons.
>   He removes kings and sets up kings.
> He gives wisdom to the wise,
>   and knowledge to those who have understanding.
> He reveals the deep and secret things.
>   He knows what is in the darkness,
>   and the light dwells with him.
> I thank you and praise you,
>   O God of my fathers,
> who have given me wisdom and might,
>   and have now made known to me what we desired of you;
>   for you have made known to us the king's matter."

Reflection: Giving all credit to God, Daniel does indeed reveal the king's dream to him and gives the interpretation. This staves off the king's execution order. But before any of this occurs, Daniel first takes time to praise the Almighty. He does this before he reveals the supernatural insight God gave him about the king's dream, which he must do to save his life.

Have we ever been so grateful to God that we wrote a psalm of praise to him? More to the point, do we even remember to thank him for his answers to our requests?

May our prayers overflow with thanksgiving to the Almighty for his many blessings.

Psalm 202:

King Nebuchadnezzar's Proclamation

Daniel 4:3, 34, and 35

Another time King Nebuchadnezzar writes an open letter to everyone. He addresses it to all nations and the people of every language who live on earth. Yes, that's everyone.

This letter is a testimony of what happened to him. This time it's another dream that has perplexed the king, and Daniel again interprets it.

Daniel proclaims that Nebuchadnezzar will be driven away from people and live with wild animals for seven years. When Nebuchadnezzar at last acknowledges that God is sovereign over all kingdoms, he will be restored to his throne.

Everything happens as Daniel predicted, but not right away.

One year later Nebuchadnezzar swells with pride over his greatness and his accomplishments. Immediately God declares judgment on Nebuchadnezzar, just as Daniel prophesied.

Seven years later Nebuchadnezzar's sanity returns, and he praises God. He covers all these events in his letter to the people. He includes two sections that celebrate God's power and sovereignty as a psalm of praise.

> How great are his signs!
> How mighty are his wonders!
> His kingdom is an everlasting kingdom.
> His dominion is from generation to generation . . .
>
> for his dominion is an everlasting dominion,
> and his kingdom from generation to generation.
> All the inhabitants of the earth are reputed as nothing;
> and he does according to his will in the army of heaven,
> and among the inhabitants of the earth;
> and no one can stop his hand,
> or ask him, "What are you doing?"

Reflection: Nebuchadnezzar—the enemy who conquered and deported God's people—makes a shocking declaration of God. Though a most unlikely person to praise God, he does so in a way that rivals some of the Psalms of God's followers. And proclaiming this before all peoples is just as startling.

How do we respond when someone we view as evil and far away from God makes an unexpected statement that exalts him? Do we find it easier to accept God's mercy for ourselves than for other people?

May we see our world through God's perspective.

Psalm 203:

King Darius's Proclamation

Daniel 6:26–27

After Nebuchadnezzar dies, Daniel continues to serve subsequent rulers, which has now passed to King Darius. Daniel has risen in power, but he also has many detractors from the ranks of the advisors who serve under him and his two counterparts. They seek to discredit him and remove him from his position. To their amazement, they find Daniel to be without fault. Their only option is to use his faith against him.

They form a plan. They trick Darius into issuing a decree declaring that for thirty days no one may pray to anyone but the king. The punishment for breaking this decree is to be thrown into a den of lions. The edict is irreversible.

They know that the devout Daniel will continue to pray to God. Then they can accuse Daniel of breaking this law.

Everything works as planned. Though distressed by the situation, Darius is bound by his own law and must follow through. He orders that Daniel be thrown to the lions for a gruesome death.

But God shuts the lions' mouths and protects Daniel. The next morning Darius rushes to the den and is relieved to find Daniel still alive. He orders Daniel be removed and for his detractors to take his place. The hungry lions kill them all.

Darius issues a decree that everyone in his kingdom must fear and revere the God of Daniel. This is Darius's psalm of affirmation:

> "for he is the living God,
>   and steadfast forever.
> His kingdom is that which will not be destroyed.
>   His dominion will be even to the end.
> He delivers and rescues.
>   He works signs and wonders in heaven and in earth,
>   who has delivered Daniel from the power of the lions."

Reflection: Daniel's exemplary work earned him the appreciation of kings and the disdain of his peers. His dedicated work made them look bad, and they didn't like it.

Do we conduct our life and our work without fault? Is our dedication to God the only way anyone could accuse us? When laws limit our faith practice will we comply or worship God regardless of the consequences?

May we live a faultless life before our accusers.

Psalm 204:

Mary's Psalm of Praise

Luke 1:46–55

We now transition from the Old Testament, which anticipates the coming Messiah, to the New Testament, which focuses on the Messiah, Jesus. We aptly begin with the events leading up to his birth.

Young Mary receives startling news. While she's engaged to Joseph, an angel greets her as someone whom God favors highly. He tells her that, though a virgin, she will become pregnant by supernatural Holy Spirit power. She will give birth to a son. And not just any son but the Son of God.

This perplexes Mary, as it would anyone, but she accepts the angel's words.

She travels to meet her relative Elizabeth, who's also expecting. She's carrying the baby who will become John the Baptist. Elizabeth, filled with the Holy Spirit, blesses Mary and her unborn child. And the unborn John leaps for joy in his mother's womb at the sound of Mary's voice.

Mary then praises God for who he is and what he is doing.

> "My soul magnifies the Lord.
> My spirit has rejoiced in God my Savior,
> for he has looked at the humble state of his servant.
> For behold, from now on, all generations will call me blessed.
> For he who is mighty has done great things for me.
> Holy is his name.
> His mercy is for generations and generations on those who fear him.
> He has shown strength with his arm.
> He has scattered the proud in the imagination of their hearts.
> He has put down princes from their thrones,
> and has exalted the lowly.
> He has filled the hungry with good things.
> He has sent the rich away empty.
> He has given help to Israel, his servant, that he might remember mercy,

as he spoke to our fathers,
to Abraham and his offspring forever."

Reflection: Though Mary had questions about the angel's shocking message, she accepted the proclamation in faith, as God's humble servant.

If God sent an angel to us, how would we respond? Would we embrace the courier's words, no matter how perplexing? Or would we reject the message because it sounded preposterous?

When God speaks to us through others, through the Bible, and through the Holy Spirit, what is our reaction? Do we accept the message through faith or reject it through logic?

May we hear God when he speaks and believe what he says.

Psalm 205:

Zechariah's Prophetic Psalm of Praise

Luke 1:68–79

Zechariah and his wife Elizabeth are far beyond their childbearing years, yet Zechariah prays for the impossible. An angel shows up and tells Zechariah that God has heard his prayers and will answer them by giving him a son. The Holy Spirit will fill the boy, who will point people back to God and prepare them for what will happen next.

Zechariah, however, doubts the angel's promise and loses his ability to speak. Even so, Elizabeth miraculously gets pregnant and has a son, just as the angel foretold.

While Mary (see "Psalm 204: Mary's Psalm of Praise") questioned God's message without consequence, Zechariah questioned the angel's promise and lost his ability to talk. We could claim that God was unfair, treating people differently for what seems like the same situation.

Yet who are we to question the Almighty? (See "Psalm 179: Job Speaks to God.") The perspective of God is different than ours. While we see things from our singular point of view, God has a big-picture outlook.

Regardless, all ends well for Zechariah. At John's circumcision, when it comes time to name their son, Zechariah uses a writing tablet to confirm that the boy's name is to be John. Then Zechariah's speech returns.

The first words out of his mouth are praises to God.

> "Blessed be the Lord, the God of Israel,
> for he has visited and redeemed his people;
> and has raised up a horn of salvation for us in the house of his servant David
> (as he spoke by the mouth of his holy prophets who have been from of old),
> salvation from our enemies and from the hand of all who hate us;
> to show mercy toward our fathers,
> to remember his holy covenant,
> the oath which he swore to Abraham our father,
> to grant to us that we, being delivered out of the hand of our enemies,
> should serve him without fear,
> in holiness and righteousness before him all the days of our life.

And you, child, will be called a prophet of the Most High;
for you will go before the face of the Lord to prepare his ways,
to give knowledge of salvation to his people by the remission of their sins,
because of the tender mercy of our God,
by which the dawn from on high will visit us,
to shine on those who sit in darkness and the shadow of death;
to guide our feet into the way of peace."

Reflection: Zechariah's psalm of praise looks at God's Old Testament promise of a Messiah and connects that with John, who will grow up to be a prophet and prepare the way for Jesus.

Are we able to see God's plans in our present reality? Can we praise him now for a future yet to occur?

May our praise to God be future focused, as well as celebrating his past and present blessings.

Psalm 206:

An Angel Chorus

Luke 2:14

At this point we've had two amazing pregnancies, first Zechariah and Elizabeth's and then Mary's, through the Holy Spirit. At John's birth, Zechariah praises God. At the birth of Mary's son, Jesus, an angel chorus chants a song of praise:

> "Glory to God in the highest,
> on earth peace, good will toward men."

Reflection: While most people have never seen an angel—at least not that they're aware of—meeting one in person would be most surprising. How much more awesome an experience to hear a large choir of angels praising God.

Though we may not yet be able to praise God like his angels did when Jesus was born, we one day will. Until then, what should we do to make our praise of God be the best it can be? Are there habits we should stop? Are there new actions we should start?

May we always praise God to the best of our abilities.

Psalm 207:

Simeon Praises God

Luke 2:29–32

After Jesus's birth, Mary and Joseph take him to the temple to dedicate him to God (see Exodus 13:2, 12). Simeon greets them at the temple courts.

God has assured him that he will not die until he sees the promised Savior. Directed by the Holy Spirit, Simeon heads off to the temple. There he meets Jesus. He holds the baby in his arms and praises God for fulfilling his promise to him—and to all people.

"Now you are releasing your servant, Master,
according to your word, in peace;
for my eyes have seen your salvation,
which you have prepared before the face of all peoples;
a light for revelation to the nations,
and the glory of your people Israel."

Reflection: Simeon believed what God promised him. And when God said to go to the temple, Simeon obeyed.

What has God promised us, either through his Word or the Holy Spirit? Are we waiting for it in faithful expectation? How will we respond when it occurs?

May we have a strong faith, a listening heart, and an obedient spirit.

Psalm 208:

Hosanna

John 12:13

Our story of Jesus now jumps ahead some three decades to the end of his earthly ministry.

His time in our world is winding down. He travels with his disciples into Jerusalem, where he will celebrate the Passover with them and institute the practice of Holy Communion. In addition to John 12:13, Jesus's triumphal procession also appears in Matthew 21:9 and Mark 11:9–10, which Psalm 118:25–26 prophetically foretold.

As Jesus makes his way into the city, the crowd lines his path and shouts their praise to him. The people belt out their boisterous psalm of adoration to Jesus:

> "Hosanna! Blessed is he who comes in the name of the Lord, the King of Israel!"

Reflection: Though the crowds praise him on this day, they will call for his death just a few days later. We don't know how many of the same people were present at both events, but we can assume there was some overlap, perhaps quite a bit. This shows us how fickle people are. Too many simply follow the crowd.

Is our praise of Jesus sincere, or do we just do what everyone else does? Is our commitment to him unwavering, or do we sometimes turn on him?

May our hosannas never end and never falter.

Psalm 209:

The Hymn of Christ

Philippians 2:6–11

This passage in Paul's letter to the Philippian church stands as a grand statement of who Jesus is and what he did for us. It is a concise, yet profound, theological statement that we would do well to contemplate and meditate on.

This passage, however, may not have been Paul's own words but instead the lyrics of one of the church's earlier hymns, which Bible scholars now call "The Hymn of Christ."

This is a passage to take in slowly, investing time to digest its words and deliberate on them. Given all it contains, it's also an ideal passage to memorize.

> [Jesus], who, existing in the form of God, didn't consider equality with God a thing to be grasped, but emptied himself, taking the form of a servant,

> being made in the likeness of men. And being found in human form, he humbled himself, becoming obedient to the point of death, yes, the death of the cross. Therefore God also highly exalted him, and gave to him the name which is above every name, that at the name of Jesus every knee should bow, of those in heaven, those on earth, and those under the earth, and that every tongue should confess that Jesus Christ is Lord, to the glory of God the Father.

Reflection: Jesus stands at the center of Christianity. His death on the cross is the ultimate sin sacrifice to end all sacrifices and reinstate us into right relationship with Father God. He is our purpose for living, our reason for hope, and our position in the kingdom of God—both now and into eternity.

How often do we praise Jesus for who he is? How often do we thank him for saving us?

May we keep Jesus central in all aspects of our life: what we do, what we say, and even what we think.

Thank you, Jesus, for who you are and what you did.

Psalm 210:

Holy, Holy, Holy

Revelation 4:8

We'll wrap up our consideration of other psalms in the Bible with nine passages from the amazing book of Revelation.

To emphasize that something is important, the Bible repeats it. It's like adding an exclamation point to it. The Bible repeats the most significant of words three times. That's like adding *two* exclamation points.

The only word reiterated three times in the Bible is the word *holy*, as in "holy, holy, holy."

Does this sound familiar? We first encountered this threefold repetition in the book of Isaiah, with angels worshiping God as holy, holy, holy. (See "Psalm 182: Angels Sing Praise.")

We now encounter it again, this time from John in his epic revelation from God. Just as with Isaiah, we don't know if God reveals this scene through a vision or if John's spirit rises into heaven to witness it. Maybe it's both, with the former giving way to the latter.

Regardless, the Bible again records four living creatures, who sound a lot like angels, endlessly chanting their praise to God, over and over, day and night, without rest. Just like the angels in Isaiah's day, these celestial beings also chant that God is "holy, holy, holy."

I wonder if the angels have been chanting this continuously from the time of Isaiah to the time of John. If so, I suspect they're still singing it today.

In John's version, however, they have a different concluding phrase. It emerges as a distinct yet profound psalm of adoration to God:

> "Holy, holy, holy is the Lord God, the Almighty, who was and who is and who is to come!"

Reflection: In addition to proclaiming God's holiness, the angels' words confirm three things about him. First, he is Lord. Second, he is Almighty (omnipotent, that is, all-powerful). And third, he is eternal, existing in time past, present, and future. The angels confirm that our eternal, Almighty, Lord God is the most holy of all.

Are we willing to affirm God as holy, holy, holy? How does the confirmation that God is Lord, Almighty, and eternal adjust our view of him and our response to him?

May we celebrate God as holy and the sole recipient of our praise.

Psalm 211:

Worthy

Revelation 4:11

After the four living creatures proclaim glory, honor, and thanks to God, he reveals more of heaven to John.

Next, we see twenty-four elders bow before God as he sits on his throne. They worship him, the one who lives for eternity. They present their crowns—representing their authority and power—to him and worship him.

> "Worthy are you, our Lord and God, the Holy One, to receive the glory, the honor, and the power, for you created all things, and because of your desire they existed, and were created!"

Reflection: The four living creatures and the twenty-four elders worship God as holy and worthy.

Do we worship God as holy and worthy? Do our attitudes and actions confirm that we believe God is holy and worthy or contradict it? How can we more appropriately worship God?

May we worship God in spirit and in truth (John 4:23–24).

Psalm 212:

A New Song

Revelation 5:9–10

Next, the four living creatures and the twenty-four elders sing a new song to God. Along with the book of Revelation, there are other verses that talk about singing a new song to God (see Psalm 98:1 and Isaiah 42:10). But this passage is the only one that records the words of a new song.

> "You are worthy to take the book
>   and to open its seals:
> for you were killed,
>   and bought us for God with your blood
>   out of every tribe, language, people, and nation,
> and made us kings and priests to our God,
>   and we will reign on the earth."

Reflection: Singing a new song to God is the gift of giving him something fresh, something alive. Offering him what is new is giving him our best. Presenting him with what is old, however, offers used—even perhaps worn out—words. God deserves better.

Do we like to sing new songs of praise to our Lord? Or are we more content to sing old hymns and choruses, the ones we like and are comfortable with?

May we give him our best as we praise him.

Psalm 213:

The Angel Chorus

Revelation 5:12

With the four living creatures and the twenty-four elders singing their new song to God, an angel chorus of millions joins in.

Imagine more than a million angels singing this psalm of praise to Jesus:

> "Worthy is the Lamb who has been killed to receive the power, wealth, wisdom, strength, honor, glory, and blessing!"

Reflection: Jesus, who died for us, is worthy to offer himself as the ultimate sin sacrifice. This psalm lists seven things he deserves to receive:

1. Power
2. Wealth
3. Wisdom

4. Strength
5. Honor
6. Glory
7. Blessing

In the Bible, the number seven represents God, completeness, and perfection. Jesus is God's complete perfection.

Do we appreciate Jesus as being worthy to die for us? Do we see Jesus as God's complete perfection?

May our perception of Jesus match what Scripture says about him.

Psalm 214:

Everyone Joins In

Revelation 5:13

We have a rising crescendo of voices praising God. We started with four living creatures. Then the twenty-four elders joined in, followed by millions of angels. But there's more.

Every creature in heaven and earth lends their voice to produce the ultimate praise team, building up to an unprecedented surge of worship.

> "To him who sits on the throne, and to the Lamb be the blessing, the honor, the glory, and the dominion, forever and ever! Amen!

Reflection: The book of Psalms says, "Let everything that has breath praise Yah!" (Psalm 150:6). We may perceive this passage as hyperbole—an idealized and unattainable goal—but in the book of Revelation we see it as a future reality. This may be one small way that Jesus fulfills the Old Testament, turning an exaggeration into actuality.

Praise Jesus!

This final group of worshipers ascribe to Jesus blessing, honor, glory, and dominion. The first three of these—blessing, honor, and glory—are part of the angels' refrain in the preceding verse. The added word is dominion. All people acknowledge Jesus's dominion—that is, his rule and authority—forever and ever.

What does Jesus's eternal rule mean to us? How might it influence us today?

May we anticipate spending eternity with Jesus.

Psalm 215:

Salvation

Revelation 7:10, 12

Our exploration of heaven, courtesy of John's revelation, continues. Next, we see a great multitude—too numerous to count and from every nation and people group—adorned in white robes crying out their song of praise to God.

Not only do these people hail from every country but they also represent every language. Imagine each person praising God in their own tongue. What a beautiful melding of languages to present their highest praise.

> "Salvation be to our God, who sits on the throne, and to the Lamb!"

The angels, elders, and four living creatures all bow down and worship. They proclaim their affirmation to what the great multitude said and to God.

> "Amen! Blessing, glory, wisdom, thanksgiving, honor, power, and might, be to our God forever and ever! Amen."

Reflection: The angels give seven words to God:

1. Blessing
2. Glory
3. Wisdom
4. Thanksgiving
5. Honor
6. Power
7. Might

This parallels Jesus's list from "Psalm 213: The Angel Chorus," with five words being an exact match. This reminds us that Jesus is, in fact, God.

Do we think of Jesus merely as a wise man who lived a good life? Or do we recognize him as God who came to us in human form to bring about our salvation?

May our worship of Jesus find inspiration from John's revelation of what happens in heaven.

Psalm 216:

Thanksgiving and Judgment

Revelation 11:15, 17, and 18

As John's revelation continues, we see a seventh angel blowing his trumpet. Then an unidentified chorus cries out loudly:

> "The kingdom of the world has become the Kingdom of our Lord, and of his Christ. He will reign forever and ever!"

In response to this, the twenty-four elders bow before God and add their worship to that of the chorus.

> "We give you thanks, Lord God, the Almighty, the one who is and who was; because you have taken your great power and reigned. The nations were angry, and your wrath came, as did the time for the dead to be judged, and to give your bondservants the prophets, their reward, as well

> as to the saints, and those who fear your name, to the small and the great, and to destroy those who destroy the earth."

Reflection: When we consider judgment, we typically think of people receiving punishment, but judgment can also produce reward. Though we don't know what other rewards may await us, eternal life with Jesus is certainly the biggest and best gift of all.

Do we look forward to our final judgment with fear or anticipation? Does what awaits us when we leave this earth produce horror or hope?

May our expectation of eternity with Jesus fill us with peace and take away all dread.

Psalm 217:

A Psalm of Deliverance

Revelation 15:3–4

After the last of seven plagues completes God's wrath, John sees those who defeated the beast worshiping the Almighty. They sing the song of Moses and of Jesus.

"Great and marvelous are your works, Lord God,
the Almighty!
Righteous and true are your ways, you King of the nations.
Who wouldn't fear you, Lord,
and glorify your name?
For you only are holy.
For all the nations will come and worship before you.
For your righteous acts have been revealed."

Reflection: It's interesting that John identifies this as the song of Moses and Jesus. Why? What is the connection?

Moses and Jesus both represent deliverance.

Through Moses the people of Israel receive deliverance from Egypt, their oppressors. Through Jesus all people can receive deliverance from sin's punishment through his sacrificial death that reconciles us with Father God.

Do we take time to praise Jesus for his deliverance from our sins?

May we celebrate Jesus for who he is and what he did.

Psalm 218:

Hallelujah, the Lamb's Wedding

Revelation 19:1–7

The final passage that we'll cover in our consideration of the Bible's other psalms unfolds as an interactive medley of God-honoring worship.

It starts with a great multitude that shouts:

> "Hallelujah! Salvation, power, and glory belong to our God; for his judgments are true and righteous. For he has judged the great prostitute, who corrupted the earth with her sexual immorality, and he has avenged the blood of his servants at her hand."

In response we hear:

> "Hallelujah! Her smoke goes up forever and ever."

The twenty-four elders and four living creatures bow before God, saying:

> "Amen! Hallelujah!"

A voice from heaven agrees:

> "Give praise to our God, all you his servants, you who fear him, the small and the great!"

The great multitude adds their conclusion:

> "Hallelujah! For the Lord our God, the Almighty, reigns! Let's rejoice and be exceedingly glad, and let's give the glory to him. For the wedding of the Lamb has come, and his wife has made herself ready."

Reflection: As John's revelation winds down, our eternal future emerges in its full glory. In the spiritual realm, Jesus will prepare to marry his bride—his church, that is, you, me, and everyone who follows him. It's the ultimate marriage to the ideal groom.

How do we respond to the idea of spiritual marriage to Jesus? Though we may not feel worthy to be wedded to his perfection, remember that through him we are made right. He views us as his pure, spotless bride (2 Corinthians 11:2 and Ephesians 5:27).

What can we do to worship Jesus for what he has done? What can we do to praise him for what he will do?

May we embrace Jesus for all his past, present, and future actions.

Psalm 219:

Your Turn

We've now covered sixty-seven additional psalms scattered throughout Scripture. These provided us with an overall arc of the biblical story. We began with Moses from long ago and ended with John's future-focused look into the spiritual realm, where we will no doubt sing our "Holy, holy, holy" to God.

Yet we don't need to wait until we enter eternity to praise God, and we don't need to restrict our psalms to what we read in the Bible. These passages can inspire us to write our own psalms to God. Perhaps you already have. If so, pull them out and look at them afresh.

And if you haven't yet written a psalm to God, now is a perfect time to start.

Here's my psalm, a simple poem of my deepest thanksgiving. It's not profound and won't win any literary awards, but it stands as my genuine gift to God.

Thank you, Jesus, for loving me.

Thank you, Jesus, for dying in my place to
pay for the many things I've done wrong.
Thank you, Jesus, for saving me
and reconciling me into a right relationship with Father God.
Thank you, Jesus, for living in me and through me.
Thank you, Jesus, for sending the Holy Spirit to guide me.
Thank you, Jesus, for eternal life,
a life which starts now.
Thank you, Jesus!

Reflection: I'm an author, so writing is easy for me. If writing doesn't come as easily for you, don't despair. Your psalm doesn't need to be grand, eloquent, or even long. It just needs to come from your heart. You can do it.

And if you need some help, ask the Holy Spirit to guide your words. Write them down, and then give them back to God. Share them with others too.

The psalms, both in the Bible and from our hearts, are an ideal way to worship God and connect with him. How else can we approach God? What else can we give him as an act of adoration?

May we worship God in spirit and in truth (John 4:24). We can do so with our words and through our actions.

Amen.

For Small Groups, Sunday Schools, and Classrooms

Beyond Psalm 150 makes a great discussion guide for small groups, Sunday schools, and classrooms. Leaders can tailor this to any length of class, dividing the psalms into the number of weeks you will meet.

As you read through this book, get together periodically to discuss the questions at the end of each chapter. The leader can either use all the questions to guide your conversation or pick some to focus on.

Before beginning your discussion, pray as a group. Ask for the Holy Spirit to give insight and clarity.

When considering each chapter's questions:

- Look for how these questions can grow your understanding of the Bible and God.
- Evaluate how these questions can expand your faith perspective.

- Consider what you need to change in how you live your life.
- Ask God to help you apply what you've learned.

May God speak to you as you use this book to study these psalms and grow closer to him.

Acknowledgments

To the God of the Bible: Father, Son, and Holy Spirit, who inspires and guides me as I write. Without you, I am nothing.

My friend Patricia M. Robertson, who blogs about the Psalms and whose book *The Psalms in Light of the Lord's Prayer* motivated me to move forward with this project.

My wife, who prays blessings for my writing each morning.

My assistant Shara, who helps me with my other work so that I have more time to write.

My online mentor Joanna Penn, who teaches and encourages me in writing and publishing.

My mastermind groups, for keeping me on track and moving forward.

My beta readers Beth Gordon, Mike Roberto, Pammers Amende, and Patricia M. Robertson, who helped shape and fine-tune this book.

And you, part of my dear tribe, who read *Beyond Psalm 150*. May God speak to you and bless you through these other psalms in the Bible as we travel together on our journey with Jesus.

About Peter DeHaan

Peter DeHaan, PhD, wants to change the world one word at a time. His books and blog posts discuss God, the Bible, and church, geared toward spiritual seekers and church dropouts. Many people feel church has let them down, and Peter seeks to encourage them as they search for a place to belong.

But he's not afraid to ask tough questions or make religious people squirm. He's not trying to be provocative. Instead, he seeks truth, even if it makes people uncomfortable. Peter urges Christians to push past the status quo and reexamine how they practice their faith in every part of their lives.

Peter earned his doctorate, awarded with high distinction, from Trinity College of the Bible and Theological Seminary. He lives with his wife in beautiful Southwest Michigan and wrangles crossword puzzles in his spare time.

Peter's a lifelong student of Scripture. He wrote the 700-page website ABibleADay.com to encourage people to explore the Bible, the greatest book ever written. His popular blog, at PeterDeHaan.com, addresses biblical Christianity to build a faith that matters.

Read his blog, receive his newsletter, and learn more at PeterDeHaan.com.

If you liked *Beyond Psalm 150,* please leave a review online. Your review will help others discover this book and encourage them to read it too. That would be amazing.

Thank you.

Peter DeHaan's Books

For a complete, up-to-date list of Peter's books, go to PeterDeHaan.com/books.

The Dear Theophilus series:

- *That You May Know: A 40-Day Devotional Exploring the Life of Jesus from the Gospel of Luke*
- *Tongues of Fire: 40 Devotional Insights for Today's Church from the Book of Acts*
- *For Unto Us: 40 Prophetic Insights About Jesus, Justice, and Gentiles from the Prophet Isaiah*
- *Return to Me: 40 Prophetic Teachings about Unfaithfulness, Punishment, and Hope from the Minor Prophets*
- *I Hope in Him: 40 Insights About Moving from Despair to Deliverance through the Life of Job*
- *Living Water: 40 Reflections on Jesus's Life and Love from the Gospel of John*
- *Love Is Patient: 40 Devotional Gems and Bible Study Truths from Paul's Letters to the Corinthians*

The 52 Churches series:

- *52 Churches: A Yearlong Journey Encountering God, His Church, and Our Common Faith*

- *The 52 Churches Workbook: Becoming a Spiritual Community that Matters*
- *More Than 52 Churches: The Journey Continues*
- *The More Than 52 Churches Workbook: Pursue Christian Community and Grow in Our Faith*
- *Visiting Online Church: A Journey Exploring Effective Digital Christian Community*

The Bible Bios series:

- *Women of the Bible: The Victorious, the Victims, the Virtuous, and the Vicious*
- *The Friends and Foes of Jesus: Discover How People in the New Testament React to God's Good News*

Other books:

- *Jesus's Broken Church: Reimagining Our Sunday Traditions from a New Testament Perspective*
- *Woodpecker Wars: Celebrating the Spirituality of Everyday Life*
- *Martin Luther's 95 Theses: Celebrating the Protestant Reformation in the 21st Century*
- *How Big Is Your Tent? A Call for Christian Unity, Tolerance, and Love*

Be the first to hear about Peter's new books and receive updates at PeterDeHaan.com/updates.

Printed in Great Britain
by Amazon

38335477R00139